20/10.

Providence Place

Providence Place

ANIMALS IN A LANDSCAPE

Jacky Gillott

Line drawings by Jane Percival

The Leisure Circle

for
my parents

I

IN THE BACK OF MY OLD MORRIS THE TWO CATS, EACH clawing desperately at the lid of its wicker basket, yowled and released abominable gases.

It was a relief to see the dark slabs of Stonehenge leaning against a wide and pinkening sky; from here only another hour or so's journey. I lowered both windows to their utmost and made fruitless, soothing noises.

As I accelerated across the smooth, exposed rise of Salisbury Plain the cats remained uncomforted. They recognized that this was a longer journey than any they had made before and were full of angry apprehension. Their apprehension fed mine. The whole undertaking began to seem absurd and although I kept up a solicitous burbling that I doubt the cats could hear above the rush of wind (of both kinds), I wondered whether my appetite for impulsive changes of direction had, on this occasion, been insanely indulged. Somewhere ahead, my children Matthew and Daniel sat in the back of my husband's car. Did he, John, entertain similar doubts? Were my sons squalling as mournfully as the two cats? For them, this move away from the home they knew best, from the school and the friends that formed the web of their lives, could have none of the compensatory excitement that spasmodically wormed its way through me.

It was no good telling myself it had largely been done for them. The desire that they should grow up in a place whose seasons and contours and community would give them a fundamental sense of time and place that nothing thereafter could wholly blur might simply strike them as a brutal uprooting.

The desperate clamour of the cats was very undermining. They strained and rasped against their wicker lids. "There, there," I said feebly.

The older of the two cats, Tiger, had arrived on the occasion of my sons' joint birthday party two years previously. He had presented himself, so it had seemed then, as a gift. With hindsight I realise he was laying claim to our kingdom.

Tiger Lil as he was called until it was observed that he was neutered rather than female, had advanced across the lawn, curled himself twice around an unoccupied leg and studied the children at play before deciding that the territory would suit him admirably. Although nothing could sound more ordinary than a tabby cat, Tiger's markings, his lithe and princely movements, and his lofty self-assurance impress themselves immediately on any eye as well above the ordinary. He is the kind of cat who, should he leap on one's lap and settle there, conveys so intense a feeling of flattery that the owner of the lap, even one who describes himself as a cat-hater, dares not move. This, despite the fact that having Tiger on one's lap is an excruciatingly painful experience. After circling, then stretching his full length along thigh or chest, he will, with a leisurely pleasure, bury the claws of first one paw then the other as deeply into one's flesh as he is

8

able. For this exercise he best appreciates bare flesh and will, with royal ingenuity, find some however well clothed you think you are: the neck, maybe, below the ear or the tiny gap between the buttons on a man's shirt. Here, in this small crevice of discovered skin, he will sink claws sharpened by a long heritage of hunting, to the rumbling sound of a purr so deep, so sensual, so autocratic that his victim lies transfixed by the honour done him.

I have seen visitors sitting at my dinner table, their faces contorted by pain, frozenly staring at the air above my head, and known that it is not my food but my favourite cat which is causing discomfort in their lower abodmen. Any offer to remove him is met by the agonised reply that it is perfectly all right, thank you. Tiger's usurping of one's lap is as resistible as Attila's descent on Rome.

His contemptuous disapproval of Aurora, when she first arrived, was expressed by his leaving home for a week. It was not an act of desertion or cowardice. It was an ultimatum. Me or *that*.

For once, because the children were so beguiled by the small, tawny puff of hair Aurora then was, we held out against him. Tiger returned home, head and tail held high, walking in a measured fashion. His solution was to ignore the kitten, behaving as though something so small was beyond the power of his large green eyes to see, then, without warning, he could enjoy an abrupt onslaught of tooth and claw just long enough to establish a rule of terror. Once Aurora was under the sofa or the spare-room bed, Tiger would elaborately wash himself as a prelude to eating any remnant of food or drink that might have been hers.

As she grew into a long-haired, sharp-eyed marmalade cat with a tail which she trailed like a starlet's careless stole, Aurora settled for indoor warmth and languor. Unlike Tiger, whose arrival on the lap was as rare as it was momentous, she sprawled permanently on laps and cushions as close as possible to the tip of somebody's burning cigarette, inhaling their expelled smoke with an air of ecstasy, eyes closed, pink nose quivering. She was, in some ways, a rather silly cat: lazy,

9

glamorous and too swift to scuttle when Tiger launched one of his terrorist attacks. Given her susceptibilities, I feared this move might reduce her to a swooning kind of horror. Tiger was the one more likely to run away. I could imagine him, a lean dart on the horizon, heading back across the compass points. A merciless and efficient predator, he would live. No question about that. But without Tiger we should be without our talisman. A thief, a liar, able to pass through locked doors at night, Tiger has the magic, the immortality of the survivor. We needed him.

The slope of the hills became less vast and naked. Wiltshire has the nudity of an old torso. It reclines, stripped, marked by earlier living. Tumuli, earthworks, whorled defences, push up beneath the pale, cropped green and gingery, flint-strewn soil. The colours are soft. Milky, sometimes.

Soon, the darker, coniferous ridge of Penselwood and Brewham Forest rose on my right. I turned off, down narrower, deepening roads overhung by trees. (I was to leave the cats in our new home and then return to Mere for an overnight stop with the family before our furniture arrived on the following day.)

The course of the road was not yet familiar and made me change down awkwardly. The big stone gateposts on the left, I *did* remember, and then down. Down and round, under the railway bridge, past the fine fifteenth-century church with its great tower, on beside the one remaining abbey wall, past the school and down Plox, a name nobody can satisfactorily translate.

Providence Place.

The cats moaned as the car tilted steeply uphill. Never had I needed a name to carry so much weight. Providence, I prayed, had brought us here.

Six months previously, on a slate-coloured January day I had been taking a turn round a Parisian pond, trying to suppress a sense of misgiving.

My companions, Jack and Tania Osterley, flanked me as

we trailed after the others who were rapidly disappearing over an ornamental bridge bent, it seemed, on yet another circuit of the flat grey gardens. The Parisians, well wrapped against the cold, earnestly played ball games with their children.

"Yes," said Jack Osterley, "it's the psycho-therapy angle that really excites me."

My heart drooped.

"Absolutely," Tania agreed with pale but undoubted warmth. "It's helped us tremendously already."

My shoes seemed to fill with gloom.

The following morning we were to visit the Osterleys' apartment in the centre of Paris. I had been promised that Jack's skilful conversions would impress me profoundly. I let him talk on eagerly about psycho-therapy, withholding both argument and judgment until both could be exercised in the light of his other, more practical, enthusiasms. A good carpenter-cum-builder was not to be dismissed. As we had gone round the group earlier in the day asking each in turn what skills he or she had to offer the commune, it had become painfully clear that keenness was not equalled by know-how.

Robin Clarke (once editor of *Science Journal*, but then working on a two-year contract with the UN in Paris) was not deterred. Robin and his wife Janine had been the ones responsible for assembling the group and getting discussions under way. Old friends of ours, I couldn't help recalling, as we returned to their high-ceilinged French house for tea (fond as I am of Robin and deeply admiring of his capacity to achieve things), one or two other instances when I'd felt his judgment of people was marginally misplaced. Unfairly, the margin grew as I considered those instances. No, I told myself, I must wait until I'd seen Jack's conversions.

All the same, as I looked around at the disparate characters, some complete strangers, some only acquaintances who had gathered together to discuss ways of spending their future lives together, I became keenly aware of my natural incapacity to live and work in groups. It is, I think, a temperamental failing of most only children but I had, until that

11

moment when we passed cups to one another in tones of subdued politeness, firmly believed that the work the commune intended to do – research into alternative technologies – was of such importance that it would transcend little human differences.

Now, as one young man produced equations and diagrams of stunning complexity I became drearily aware that not one person had made a worthwhile joke all day (only the Clarkes and ourselves appeared remotely aware of our ludicrous side), I concluded that Jack Osterley's do-it-yourself would have to be spectacular.

In a sense, it was.

We seemed to climb ten narrow flights of stone steps to reach the apartment. My children thought it magnificent and promptly climbed the wooden ladder that reached up to an exposed sleeping gallery high in the roof. They sat there, legs swinging over the edge, threatening to throw the Osterleys' pillows down; a prospect that seemed to harass the Osterleys who had no children of their own as yet. I ignored the little stir of ill-feeling and turned my attention to the structural problems the conversion had created. They had been cleverly resolved by the support of two vast polystyrene-covered pillars of lumpy, slimy aspect.

As Tania spooned out stew, they assumed larger and larger proportions, those pillars. I couldn't take my eyes off them.

I know it is foolish and cruel to judge a man by his pillars, but taken in conjunction with the psycho-therapy, they spoke volumes. Their message was stridently clear. Forget it, sunshine, they said.

And so, although we spent months limping through waterlogged meadows looking at suitable farms in Wales on behalf of the commune, our hearts had gone out of the venture. The pillars had struck John with exactly the same force. Guiltily, we extracted ourselves from the scheme and somehow, in June, within three weeks of first seeing the place by complete accident, we had come to Providence Place.

12

The car bounced from one irregular rut to another up the steep hill. The cats intensified their wailing. When I stopped and switched off the engine, they fell guardedly silent.

Because it sits on a small hill of its own, the house looks larger than it really is. Its proportions are actually quite small and because of the thickness of the stone walls, the interior rooms are more cramped than one would imagine from the outside. Plainly, our furniture was not going to fit.

A low, warm sun still shone on the golden stone of the cliff wall that rises at the back of the house and continues some fifty yards to the left of it. The cliff, from which the stone of the house had been hewn over two hundred years before was heavily clad in ivy and honeysuckle. It contained, so I'd been told, a cave used for storing rubbish by past owners and only fairly recently sealed off. The small area of lawn beneath the cliff had been lovingly tended, a neat green square edged at one side with Canterbury bells and hypericum. Everything else had escaped control. Nettles, docks and tall, coarse grasses made the house appear, from the foot of the hill, to be sinking amidst a tide of growth. In two small orchards, one at either side of the slope which semi-circled the house like a long skirt, leaned ancient, unpruned cider apple trees arthritically bent. A thrush, unseen, cracked a snail against a stone. The air was thick with the suppurating stench of wild garlic whose leaves fell everywhere in cascades of green, satin ribbons.

Lifting the cat baskets from the car I carried them to the tiny greenhouse which was built into the side of the house. The panes on the door were framed with a border of stained glass. A solitary tendril of vine crept through the foundation wall of old brick and reached upward. Somebody had left a few pink and red geraniums in pots. Their scent was sharp, sweet and refreshing.

The cats glared at their surroundings without moving from the hunched positions they adopted when I put them down on the floor. Their tails whisked in uncertain, jerky displeasure. I fed them and hoped they would tolerate these surroundings for a week: during the day builders would be

13

uprooting the insides of the house. At least they had some earth in here to scratch. At least they could look out and watch our activities. I hoped fervently that the weather would stay cool so that the greenhouse wouldn't become uncomfortable, and quietly closed the door on their irascible forms.

The next day it began to rain. It rained in great vertical poles of water that blotted out whole sections of countryside and provoked a surliness in the removal men who found it impossible to manoeuvre their van up the hill. Every single item of furniture had to be carried up the fearful gradient.

The cats looked out from behind streaming panes of glass and found what they saw dismal. Indoors as I climbed over people, my clothes steaming, I, too, looked at the low, darkened rooms and passages, with foreboding. (Later I learned from Mrs Appleby, who had known this house as a child nearly seventy years ago, that it had been called Reckless, a corruption of Rack's Close, so named because the bleached linen was spread out to dry on the south-facing slope. Reckless, indeed.)

At eight, after the removal men had left, the rain eased. From the kitchen window, looking down on the patchwork of old, tiled roofs in the valley I saw rays of evening sun pierce the veils of rain. The air become iridescent. The walls and roofs of the cottages facing one another across the narrow division of a stream, glowed peach. A rainbow formed two parallel hoops across the hills.

After nightfall, I let the cats have the run of the house and they sped wildly hither and thither diving into all its dark corners, pausing fractionally over familiar furniture but choosing a crowded, windowless boxroom to sleep in. They found its furthest corner beneath cases and mattresses and piles of books and pressed their bodies as flat as they could to the floor.

Their week was up. They were to be set free.

I opened the door of the workshop which leads into the

14

greenhouse and waited, with some dread, to see how they would respond.

Tiger displayed an instant and unqualified delight in what he plainly took to be a cat's paradise. In no time at all the house was littered inside and out with the corpses of mice and shrews. Ears flattened, eyes large, he prowled in perpetual hunt and in the effort to convey his undiluted joy, he daily brought a tithe of limp warm bodies to my feet. One was a mole, velvet black with disproportionately large but perfect, clawed, pink feet. The bringing of tribute was heralded by a particular mewing note: a deep, prolonged yowl which slid into a concluding purr. When I hear that cry I put a closed door between myself and Tiger if I am not feeling strong enough to receive the gift gratefully.

Apart from the human animal, the domestic cat is the only creature that appears to kill for pleasure. Perhaps we share this interesting and unattractive attribute because our common ease of access to food and comfort – particularly in the city – leaves our killing instinct unused, unsatisfied. I was anxious to see how Aurora, a more truly decadent, indolent city cat than most, would adapt to her changed surroundings.

After remaining in a state of shock for some three weeks or so she overcame her catalepsy (an unintentional but very exact pun), deserted her cushions and absorbedly took up hunting – although she did so with characteristic languor. Unlike Tiger, who can sometimes be met in fields miles away from the house stalking his prey, Aurora remains within the three and a bit home acres and sits for hours upon a gatepost or strategic piece of fence, her plumed tail twitching in controlled anticipation as she peers into a promising burst of cow parsley beneath her. It is a most effective and labour-saving method.

As the years have passed, Aurora has become our prime rat-catcher, often preferring to sleep on a sack in the tack-room overnight instead of being indoors inside the washing basket or the airing cupboard. After one of her nights out, I am usually confronted, as I open the tack-room door to make up early morning feeds, with the headless corpse of a

15

sizeable rat. Preserving still the appetite of a petulant beauty who might, in human form, toy with a peeled grape, Aurora's chief delicacy, it seems, is nibbled brain cell of rat.

In those early months, the children and I explored the neighbouring woods, the Somerset levels, sliced across by sharply glittering rhines[1], the pyramidal tor that springs up out of those flat lands and convinces people so readily that magic encircles Glastonbury. We visited the great, dark rift of Cheddar Gorge and counted butterflies that flew in clouds off the high, tree-clad rim of Cadbury Camp. We found our bearings. From Cadbury, we could look north-west to the small blue triangle of Glastonbury Tor, south to the barer sweep of Dorset, and almost due north to Creech Hill, which rises up behind our house. Its tree-tangled crest, visible for miles, which gives it the aspect of a sleeping prehistoric beast, conceals the stones and treasures of a Romano-Celtic temple.

Closer to home, directly behind the house, before the hill gathers itself for its last dip and climb to Creech, it rises through our back paddock and the big fifteen-acre field beyond which together comprise Charley Hill. From the top of Charley, where I climb almost every day of my life, unfolds the view I love best. We have tried, friends have tried, both to photograph it and to paint it, but it isn't possible because no one section of it succumbs to framing. It circles you panoramically, starting with the gentle, elmed dome of Creech Hill, falling in the long reclining lines and curves that contain Coombe Farm and Whaddon, climbing again to the dark pelt of Brewham Forest, where Alfred's Tower[2] stands sentinel above the trees, then slips towards Redlynch, Godminster, Shepton Montague, each village distinguished by its special contours of Celtic field shapes which throw long blue shadows in the evening sun and give this part of

[1] Pronounced 'reens', the dykes that were cut to drain the peatland.
[2] Said to mark the place where Alfred gathered his troops in 879 A.D. and made his final, triumphant assault on the Danes, keeping Wessex free of their influence.

16

Somerset its characteristically horizontal planes. Then on, round to the mound of Bratton Seymour and away, westwards towards Wyke Champflower and the plain of Avalon beyond, before returning to its topmost starting point of Creech Hill. This marvellous bowl holds many interleaving, overlapping hills folding down towards the town, the most distinct of all surmounted by the dovecote, the old pigeon tower of the abbey that once stood here. Beneath it, the church tower and roofs cleave together in a long huddle of living. The train runs through the middle of the cluster, its noise enormously amplified by the reverberating valley walls. Sounds of lorries and children playing at the school rise clearly to the top of Charley, where cows graze and two buzzards sometimes circle. The inseparable aspects of peace and busy working life make this wide, enveloping view quite unlike any other.

I have stood there often, marvelling at the purity of light and making silent acknowlegment to Providence.

2

I T IS NOT EVERYBODY'S GOOD FORTUNE TO ENJOY THEIR CHILD-
hood twice over.

Somewhere, there is a photograph of me aged two astride
a plough horse on one of the Welsh farms where my mother
and I lodged during the war years. After the war when my
father returned, we lived (again on the top of a steep hill) in
a Lancashire village that looked across to the witches' hill,
Pendle. There I was taught to ride by the sister of the jockey
Jimmy Uttley. Bareback first. "See if you can stay on," she
said and slapped the rump of a small piebald pony that tore
round the field. "You have to fall off seven times before you
can ride," she said and I hurled myself off at every available
opportunity in the hope it would bring that desired skill all
the more quickly. Horses then were called Nigger and Bess

18

and Star. I loved the smell of them, the warm smell of their bedding, the smell of saddle soap on old, blackened leather. It didn't matter that they made me sneeze and brought me out in terrible rashes, if I heard the distant sound of hooves on the road I would run until I found the horse and patted it and gave it the furry piece of carrot that was always to be found at the bottom of one of my pockets.

We moved again, to a northern seaside town and there, at an age when one of today's girls would fret over the latest hairstyle and be in love with a rock star, I moved at an un-rhythmic pace along the tidy pavements, knees raised high, brown gymslip flapping, hands held carefully before me lightly curled round imaginary reins. I tossed my head and clicked my tongue. I snorted faintly and swerved, distended eyeballs fixed on a brightly painted gatepost or squeaking pram. I was a horse.

Not *merely* a horse. A horse and rider, fused like Epona the Gaulish horse-goddess or Riannon her counterpart in Welsh and Irish myth. They say the White Horse of Uffington was cut into the hillside to signify the cult of the horse-goddess, but I in my gymslip knew nothing of that. To the probable bewilderment of those who peered from the back bedrooms of their boarding houses down into the yard of the house which we, as top floor flat-dwellers, were allowed to use, I put myself over a course of jumps made out of brooms, rakes, upturned buckets, flower pots and a clothes line. Even more puzzling to the sentry of the net curtain, I daresay, were the moment when I (the horse) refused a jump and had to be thwacked with an imaginary stick by the rider (myself). Later, I would put myself away in a real stable, one of the yard's most treasured outbuildings. It had an old iron hay rack fixed to the wall and an exposed loft I could reach by climbing a ladder. It was a very important, very private place.

Almost as beautiful as the stable was the beach where I galloped headlong over hard, rippled sand. My sandals thundered like the real thing. A crust of salt formed on my upper lip. I jumped the breakwater and sailed over the big black iron girders under the pier (where many a grave and courteous fellow would open his mackintosh like a pair of wings and reveal a peculiar aspect of adulthood to the leaping and largely indifferent horse). Occasionally I failed to clear the girders and have small, shiny dips and scoops on my shins to this day that bear witness to my falls.

Up the dunes, legs toiling in the sliding sand and down, in two bounds, with a whinny of delight. Sometimes, over-exuberant, I would buck myself off and lie awhile in the warm, gritty substance: the sand, the thin glint of sea, the pale canopy of cloud which stretched for miles. I could gallop and gallop leaping over tiny inlets and brown fans of seaweed. I have never been happier.

In a red cash book I wrote down the names, heights, ages and colouring of all my horses. They numbered around forty. My favourite, the one I rode most consistently, was a bay hunter type with a Roman nose called Randal.

Sometimes I was able to persuade my friend Christina Fazackerly to come riding with me but she was less enthusiastic than I, and after she grew fur under her arms (it gave off an exciting musky smell which we considered with the solemnity of wine-fanciers) her interest waned entirely. She took up amateur dramatics and eventually joined the Women's Royal Air Force, where she won awards for things and got her picture in the local paper.

After Christina lost interest I rode alone. Apparently alone, that is. In truth I executed the *piaffes* and the *levades* of the *haute école* before audiences silent with admiration. I fought for the bit of a wall-eyed mare nobody else in the world had managed to tame and won the Show Jumper of the Year to the applause of thousands. Even now, when I have to go up to London, I walk along Regent Street on the look-out for a runaway police horse which I plan to catch in the face of on-coming traffic and ride back to the fallen police officer.

I was alone, not lonely. There was nothing pathetic about my aloneness. Only with hindsight do I realise that the totality, the lovely uninterruptedness of my hippomania had a lot to do with my being an only child. I wasn't forced into

20

it out of loneliness, although the desire for an engrossing kind of companionship was no doubt a component of the obsession. More importantly, there was no one to distract me from it with squabbling or silly games of their own. It may well be true that it has led to my being socially ungainly. I don't now snort in company but I don't seek it either. It may even be true that I fall into that category of people who prefer animals to humans (though I hope I never proclaim the fact with the kind of defiant pride I hear in the tone of confessed animal addicts. The preference says more about our defectiveness as human beings than it says for the attractiveness of animals.) When I claim I would rather face a lion in the bush than a bunch of humans in cocktail-party array I speak the truth. What does irritate me, however, is the jocular belief that little girls with a passion for horses are indulging in some form of sexual sublimation: mastering something between the legs.

It's a coarse interpretation because it mistakes the nature of the love. Hippomania resembles maternal longing more closely than direct sexual longing. It is the desire to look after something, the more demanding the better. The care and management of horses is far more consuming of effort than anything a cat or a budgie demands. It is this desire, not some infantile perversion, which gives rise to the greed for bits, martingales, boots and girths and all the other joys of a saddler's shop. As for whips and spurs, only a fool thinks they are for punishing a horse. Like a child's abacus and bricks, they are or should be – a gentle part of a horse's education, a means of guiding, part of the communication between horse and rider.

I was, in my prolonged fantasy, both horse and rider. Therein lies the sacred, special element of hippomania – the merging of the two creatures – for the horse on its own is a timid, fearful beast. Its first instinct when alarmed is not to kick or bite, but to flee. The horse, to be honest, is on the cowardly side and will gallop in terror from a flapping rick-sheet or even the sudden upward flight of goldcrests from a hedge. The miracle that erupts from the fusion of a good

21

rider and a horse is that the horse, making a gift of his complete trust to the human being gains the confidence that makes him capable of performing with a courage and brilliance that the rider is privileged to share. Such a partnership cannot be experienced by those commonly described as 'horsey'. They are too brutish and noisy. Horses dislike 'horsey' people.

I achieved this merging of purpose and spirit only in my dreams as I cantered through the sea's edge in my plimsolls. For one thing there was never any question of my parents being able to buy me a pony. We didn't, at that time own a car or even a telephone. Life in a top-floor flat meant that ambition extended no further than a tank of tropical fish. But I enjoyed my five-bob-an-hour rides along the beach to Blackpool on Sunday mornings and in the holidays I sometimes got a free ride in return for mucking out at the stables run by Irene, a large woman with henna-dyed hair and purple cheeks, who drank continual mugs of hot, black Oxo. I kept a form book on racing, comparing my selections with those of the The Scout in the *Daily Express*. I was better than The Scout. The newsagent asked me for good tips. But although I accepted that I would never ever have a horse of my own and although I contented myself most of the time with the dancing horses in my head, sometimes they were not quite enough. I wanted a real animal of some kind for myself. I stole a few dogs off the beach to have the pleasure of their possession for a short while before ringing their owners to report a stray. Sometimes I was given a small reward by these grateful owners and that was nice, but I would have preferred to keep the dogs.

One day my history mistress – a woman with the most urgent eyes I have ever seen – asked the class if anybody would like a puppy. Hands went up, mine among them. Would we ask our mothers, she said. The following day I told her my mother was very happy for me to have the puppy and the day after that he was put in my arms. He was a small black mongrel, warm and wriggly to hold. He was the next best thing to a pony. I took him home and hid him in the stable. After tea I told my mother I was going to feed my horses and escaped downstairs with as much of my tea as I could conceal in my blazer pocket. The puppy looked very small and miserable curled in one corner of the stable and I knew I would have to tell.

Bedtime came. I told my parents that there was something in the stable I wanted them to see and then, as they went downstairs, I flew to the bathroom and hung out of the window high at the top of the house watching them in the summer evening, watching to see what expression their bodies would register when they returned into view.

They liked the puppy. They said I could keep him. He was called Nicky and he galloped everywhere at my horse's heels. I taught him to jump the girders under the pier. Perhaps my parents had hoped the puppy would drive the horse out of their house since I was becoming embarassingly large for all this prancing and whinnying. But he didn't. He enjoyed my trotting and leaping and ran to the front door with delight when it was time for a ride.

One morning Nicky foamed at the mouth and rushed round and round the kitchen in a lake of his own saliva. When I came home from school he was dead. To distract me from my weeping my mother suggested I go and play tennis over a home-made net with my friend Firthy. Lamely, for a while, I did so. Then I put my racket down and started jumping over the net instead. It was a more consoling thing to do.

Dreams came very naturally in such a town. For all its decorous trimness, its miniature railway, boating lake, putting green and immaculate blue and white buses, it was a place rich in people whose grand dreams had been realised. One schoolfriend of mine lived in the house George Formby had died in. Another was Al Read's daughter.

Every summer when the big shows opened in Blackpool, the stars would rent their houses in St Annes because it was thought more select. There were no chippies visible in St. Annes. No fun fairs. There were nice rock gardens and miniature waterfalls and concerts of light music in the Floral Hall on the pier. Every Thursday in the holidays I went to the Floral Hall for the children's concert. Uncle Lionel would let you conduct the orchestra in weird-time versions of the Teddy Bears' Picnic. The old ladies wept with laughter as Uncle Lionel pulled faces behind the earnest child-conductor's back. Once I went in for a talent contest there and recited "Oh where ha' ye been Lord Randal my son/Oh where ha' ye been my handsome young man'" in a fine Scottish accent that didn't win me a prize but satisfied my pressing urge to perform in front of an audience. I quite seriously considered doing horse impersonations.

To this town came Josef Locke, Jack Warner, Diana Dors, Julie Andrews, Donald Peers and Yana with her two poodles. Sabrina, who lived in Blackpool, was then being courted by a subsequent boyfriend of mine. Less glamorous dreams had been realised too, by people who had made fortunes in Manchester – in cotton and furs – and wanted to live away from their factories. They lived in large red brick bungalows on the front where the sand blew in drifts all over their gardens. Quite a few had chauffeurs. All around me I saw dreams fulfilled on a flamboyant scale. Even mine, in some measure, were realised.

Every day a large, moustached figure, wearing a flat tweed cap and glasses, passed by our house. Sometimes – very slowly – he rode a stately bicycle. Sometimes he drove a trap with a skewbald pony between the shafts. Major Jesson, J.P. was an abrupt man, who was improbably rumoured to have a close relationship with his housekeeper. Whatever the truth of the matter he had, living in the same house, a very tall, thin, bespectacled nephew whose showjumper, Red Rover, was a well-known local celebrity. Their picture was often in the paper.

I have no clear memory of the Major ever speaking to me directly so he must have been able to divine a horse lover when he saw one from the saddle of his noble bicycle. It was his practice to visit the horse sales in Preston and buy up some of the animals that came on Irish boats for the

24

knacker's yard. He bought anything which took his fancy even when he had nowhere to put the animal, a carelessness which led to his renting the stable at the back of our house. I was put in charge of whatever appeared there.

The horses changed week by week and, since the Major never spoke to me, I never quite knew what I was going to find there when I came home from school. The only time I ever recall hearing his voice was on the afternoon I was appointed to ride a Connemara pony bareback to the station, where it was to be loaded on to the train. The Major pedalled behind me at a discreet distance. It was only when we passed the goods yard at a strong canter that I heard the Major's voice. A formidable military bellow. Continuous too, as our speed and the distance between ourselves and the station increased. The pony was round and slippery and strong. It was all I could do to stay on, let alone stop. Finally, I fell off whereupon the pony came to an obliging halt and the holiday traffic was once more able to wind its way round us. Charabancs full of staring faces, tongues locked to lollipops passed by.

After that, if there were any messages the Major's six-foot-six nephew came round with them. His school cap looked like a tiny garland on a maypole.

There were two minute Shetlands who had pulled Cinderella's coach in a pantomime, then a seventeen-hand racehorse, followed by a kindly Irish mare, followed (without warning) by another, remarkably vicious one. Unaware of the change, I went into the stable one dark evening to be both bitten and kicked in a single movement. There was a wretched, ribby animal that I, out of ignorant generosity, overfed and caused to go down with terrible colic. There was a piebald Shetland mare I could bring to a halt by putting both feet on the ground. There was a blue roan, a strawberry roan, a spotted horse, an uncut Palomino colt, as mad as his china blue eyes presaged, who reared up and tried to come down on top of me. It was an education. It was a dream nearly but not quite fulfilled – for none of these horses belonged to me, none was frankly good enough, nor in my care

25

long enough for me to school them to the point where I could truly win the trophies I still collected after clearing the tennis net or a hoe laid between two upturned flower pots.

The beasts I cared for were quiet, ordinary creatures in the main. But the collective, emblematic horse in my head was not. All my most potent longings were lodged within its equine form. It represented love, ambition, friendship, tenderness, escape, acceptance, success. It filled gaps in my experience left by the rootless uncertainty of the war years. Wherever I went, whatever else was left behind, my horse came with me. It was the wild and difficult part of the world I could just control. It was my comfort, danger and delight.

It is strange to me that today my parents live in the house where Major Jesson once lived. That their car is in the garage where his smart trap was once kept. But even harder to grasp some mornings when I wake to the sight of leaves in the window and the sound of turtledoves warbling within the tree, is the fact that I do possess a horse of my own and that I have, fleetingly, known what it is for horse and human so to combine in movement and purpose that they can become a single, intensely living form. It has been bitterly won, that precious knowledge. Perhaps that is why I cherish it so.

3

I WORKED IT OUT CAREFULLY. IT WAS JUST CONCEIVABLE.
The only thing I had ever saved for in my entire life had
become a real possibility.

We hunted through the small ads of the *Western Gazette*,
skimming the lengths of columns devoted to poultry, cattle
farm machinery, pigs . . . horses.

*Three-year-old chestnut gelding by Autumn Gold. 15.2.h.
Sound.*

We went to look him over. More importantly, though I
wasn't to realise it at the time, we went to meet his vendors,
Hugh and Lizzie Holgate.

Liz, a tiny, slimly-built woman in her forties with a handsome face and a shock of hair once a startling red, now a soft,
autumnal colour, led the horse out and trotted him up and

27

down so that we could judge whether he moved straight.

I put the reputation chestnuts have for being difficult to the back of my mind. He was a nicely-made little horse with one white sock and a white star. Liz, who had broken him that summer, lunged him over a few poles (reminiscent of my own garden rakes and flower pots) and asked us to note how freely he jumped, how nicely he curved his back. Several good eventers, she commented, had come of Autumn Gold stock.

"What would you want him for exactly?" she queried.

I looked blank. "Well, to *ride*" was the obvious but clearly inadequate answer. I sensed that I had ventured into a horse world far removed from the rough and casual riding of my Lancashire youth where the only people who could afford decent horses were the daughters of scrap merchants.

"Will you want to hunt him?" prompted Liz.

"Oh no," I said very quickly. "No, not hunt. Just hack about."

"*Not* hunt?" she echoed, with a quizzical look.

There was no explanation I could unoffendingly offer. In Lancashire we'd enjoyed Treasure Hunts and potato races across a tussocky field rented by the scruffy, local Pony Club. But we hadn't *hunted*. There was no hunting tradition in that part of the country, no tradition of breeding to hunt. Eventing, then, hadn't been heard of.

I *had* hunted once. In Hampshire, when I was seventeen. I'd been teaching O-levels to girls of sixteen at a private boarding school. The headmistress had, one autumn, hauled her ancient pony out of the field he'd occupied for the past ten years, shoved a crash hat on my head and said I mustn't miss the opportunity of a day out. At the sight of hounds, this elderly and irritable pony had shed fifteen years and taken a hold on the bit which resulted in his overtaking not only the huntsmen but hounds themselves. Even I knew this was strictly not etiquette and was most embarrassed to find myself in at the kill some moments before the Master arrived. He must have been a tolerant man for after smearing blood on both my cheeks without reproach, he presented me with

28

the mask. I'd ridden home with my bloody trophy bumping up and down upon my thigh. But that had been a long time ago. Since then, I suppose I had absorbed the townee's general disapproval of hunting. It wasn't a thing I contemplated for myself at all.

"Just to ride round the lanes, um?" Liz repeated with an expression that I was able, later, to interpret as pity for the horse. However, she had an animal to sell so she saddled him up for me to ride.

She had broken him well. He behaved beautifully although I was not, frankly, as familiar with the limitations and problems of a young horse as I should have been. My adolescent knowledge had been left unimproved and undeveloped. For the moment, though, Solomon, still sensitive to the will and the presence of Liz, carried me uncomplainingly, trotting, cantering, halting exactly as I asked him, although my wishes must have felt very oddly conveyed to him. A generalised kicking of the legs had sufficed perfectly well on my rag-bag of ponies twenty years before.

It was strange to be back in the saddle again. The only person who fits naturally on to a horse, I've concluded, is one with long, slender legs and a relatively short back nicely indented at the waist to provide a well-curved buttock. With a long straight back, no bum and short, sturdy legs I have a problem. In any event, those books or instructors who insist that the shoulders should be well back, thighs flat against the saddle, ankles relaxed and supple, heels down, toes up, don't realise that they're asking someone of my build to force everything into a position quite unnatural to it. As somebody once said to me, I have a nice seat on a horse as long as the horse is standing perfectly still. After a break of fifteen years I was distressed to find that when the horse moved my sense of balance had deserted me. My legs tended to shoot either backwards or forwards, my hands were liable to fly up and my torso tipped over the horse's mane. It *is* possible for the imperfectly built to acquire a passable seat – which simply means to be balanced and in time with the horse's movement at all phases – but it comes only with the development of muscles that are normally content to lie relatively idle. (Regular riding has given me more of a backside than I once possessed, thank heaven. Without it you feel as though you are sitting on two hard-boiled ostrich eggs).

Still, Solomon carried me with a cautious willingness. It remained only for him to be vetted as sound (there was some nasty scarring from barbed wire on the bulb of one heel) and he would be mine.

The prospect filled me with joyous disbelief. To own any horse had remained a dream. To own a quality horse, three part thoroughbred, was almost beyond my grasping. But, as soon as we had finished the necessary fencing and field shelter, the Holgates would deliver him.

John now knows all there is to know about fencing. Recently he fenced a small paddock in a single day. Then, he was just learning.

The task was made more lengthy and difficult (and, ultimately, ineffective) by attempting to drive posts into baked, summer earth. The field shelter, a rustic building, roofed and closed on three sides, also took much longer to build than was planned, for a very simple reason.

A neighbouring farmer, Joss Edwin, whose dry heifers graze the adjoining fifteen-acre field on Charley Hill, wandered into the paddock one afternoon and gazed at the monument being erected.

"Keeping elephants are you?" he asked after a thoughtful silence.

John stepped down the ladder and stood back to share Joss's view. "Elephants?" he echoed, staring at his own handiwork.

"It's a goodish height," observed Joss of the field shelter.

It is a good height. One horse standing on the back of another needn't fear for his head. Whether because of its height from the ground or the apprenticeship that went into its erection I don't know, but the roof of that field shelter, John's first attempt at building, has never ceased to give us

30

difficulty. It has leaked, fallen in and blown off with almost ritual regularity: as if its function were to remind us of our imperfect abilities.

The field shelter and fencing as good as finished, there remained one problem as far as the horse was concerned – the quality of the grazing. Amoore's paddock, as the small back field is called on old maps, had been left untreated, ungrazed and uncut for some time. By September its grasses were coarse and bleached yellow. Not even a cow would have found much to enjoy and horses are far more fastidious grazers than cows. No matter, it was space enough to move in and he would be getting enough supplementary feeding to keep him fit.

All the same, the expression on Liz Holgate's face as she led the little chestnut horse up the back lane to the field was one of undisguised alarm. Liz is quite incapable of concealing her feelings, although she thinks she does by voicing remarks which bear no relation to the lie of her features. "It will be lovely for him up here! High enough to be free of flies." Not even that was true.

Hugh is less compromised by politeness. A tall, thin man with engagingly dislocated limbs, he said forbiddingly, "You will *feed* him, won't you?"

"Of course."

He looked about critically. "I only hope he's not going to get out," he remarked.

"Sh-sh-sh." Liz delivered her husband a warning look which, because of the vast discrepancy in their heights, he was totally unable to see.

"He might get lonely." Hugh went on running huge fingers through his escaping hair and looked vaguely about for another horse.

"Oh, I'm sure he'll be fine," insisted Liz, smiling weakly through her consternation.

"Horses can be the devil on their own," mused Hugh.

We removed Solomon's halter and he careered wildly from

31

one end of the paddock to the other, stopping to snort and look pop-eyed at his new surroundings from time to time.

"Oh Christ," murmured Liz.

"Be firm with him," said Hugh. "You mustn't let a young horse mess you about or you won't be able to manage him."

My little horse, my dream, was becoming an anxiety.

He gave a flying buck, galloped another length of the paddock and whinnied urgently.

"He's just used to having other horses around," Liz tried to excuse him. "He'll settle," she said, without conviction.

We took the Holgates away and gave them a drink in the kitchen. Because our house sits on a small platform with the cliff wall rising behind it and the back paddock above, on a level with the bathroom window, it was possible to look up through the back door of the kitchen and the screen of sycamore leaves to see Solomon's legs pounding up and down. He was whinnying continually.

"Are you just going to keep the one horse?" enquired Liz, her eyes sliding upward through the green leaves outside.

Another one was out of the question.

"I hadn't thought of another one," I said feebly.

"Finish up your drink," Hugh urged his wife and launched into a critique of that morning's *Times* leader.

"If you want any advice or help, you will let me know, won't you?" said Liz. She was temporarily lending me a saddle. "Of course, he's only a baby, so I should keep lungeing him."

"Yes?" I said, blenching. I'd not done any lungeing before.

"And this winter, if were you, I should just put him away. His back will be much stronger next spring."

Put him away? That was not an expression much used in Lancashire. To be strictly honest, it was not an expression I had heard much used in Hampshire or Yorkshire either. It was not an expression I had ever heard. Dimly, I gathered it meant that one was not to ride the horse at all.

"I've got a marvellous book I could lend you," Liz was saying.

Later, I took up her offer and borrowed it.

Although in my head I rode beautifully, I had a lot to learn.

It was not sentimental of Hugh Holgate to worry about the horse being lonely. Cats and dogs aside, no animal likes to be kept on its own, particularly horses which are, after all, herd animals. Like cows, they will always attempt to join others of their own kind if they see them and nothing, not barbed wire, nor five-barred gates will prevent them.

My first outing on Solomon brought this plainly home.

It began badly with the ford. The back lane which runs downhill from the house ends in a shallow ford. This in itself might not have been a major problem but the ford immediately runs, with a sudden burst of sweetly-roaring speed, underneath a cottage (once a mill) and then continues to wind peacefully through the cottage owner's garden.

Solomon reacted to the ford like an animal who has never gazed on water before. He dug his front feet into the ground, blew at the stream suspiciously, then wheeled round for home. The performance continued for some time.

"Don't let a young horse mess you about," Hugh had warned. It is a sound warning.

A horse is considerably stronger than you are. It has no reason to do what you ask of it, beyond respecting you sufficiently to please you and respond to whatever signal you make. It can be no more than a signal. You cannot *force* a horse through water. Or over a jump or past a transporter or through a blazing hoop. One sharp tap of the whip expresses your displeasure but it cannot make the horse do anything he basically does not want to do. And he will not *want* to do anything if he feels you are unworthy of his trust.

Should you get yourself into a real fight or the horse decides to rid himself of you, the horse, most assuredly, will win. Not everybody, I think, certainly not those who complain about cruelty in racing and showjumping, realise that the relationship between a horse and its rider is based on so delicate a foundation. It is fundamentally an emotional relationship, not a question of brute mastery. Occasionally you will see a good horse who is so honest, whose early schooling has been so thoroughly absorbed, that he will go on performing well for a bully, but his distress will be apparent and he will very likely end by refusing to jump at all.

Solomon's refusal to step into the water, however, had an element of plain obstinacy in it and that was a different matter. I could not afford to give in to him. Dismounting, I attempted to lead him through the water. He leant his whole weight backwards with great determination. I became very hot and rather exasperated. But I stood firm. That is to say, I stood in the water for fully thirty minues. At some juncture it must have occurred to him that the water wasn't harming my feet in any way so it probably wouldn't harm his either. Or perhaps he just became bored. Whatever changed his mind it was very abrupt in its effect. He trotted so smartly through the ford that he soaked me from head to foot and dragged me out after him.

Half a mile further on we emerged from a lane on to the bend of a narrow but fairly busy road. Behind the wall which bordered the far side of the road, two mares with their foals began to bound towards us neighing in welcome.

A fresh and more desperate skirmish began.

Solomon refused to leave his new-found friends. Every time he wheeled back on his hocks to face them, I shortened the inside rein and whirled him in three or four tight circles to dizzy him and then push him on towards home.

He wasn't so easily fooled. Every now and then a car looped towards us, blaring angrily which did little to calm him. Both of us were sweating profusely. By this time I was not so much angry as afraid.

Tiring of the circling trick, he essayed a new method. He reared. A token rear to start with, then an almighty leap upwards into the air, half-turning as a lorry gasped round the corner.

Until this moment an element of obduracy had coloured his behaviour. That was the element I had to govern. But even his obstinacy was, in part, a loss of trust. Now, my own fear had communicated itself to him: perhaps my voice had shrilled momentarily, possibly my thighs felt like a large pair of moths fluttering against the saddle. Whatever had given me away, the game was for the moment lost. If a horse senses fright in his rider his response is always to become frightened himself and his response to fear is flight.

If I had ridden more frequently in the months before I had owned him, I would probably have had the confidence to calm him, but my nerve had gone. As he reared and reared again I was absolutely terrified of falling off, something that wouldn't even have occurred to me fifteen years before.

There was nothing for it on that dangerous corner but to dismount and lead him home. As soon as I thought it safe, I remounted but I knew in my heart of hearts that a crucial confrontation had been lost. It would take months to repair all the work Liz had put into this young horse and I had woefully undone.

So I began again at the beginning by lungeing him regularly. Lungeing means driving a horse round you in a fairly large circle on a long rein. It sounds pointless but is actually a very valuable exercise. After the initial handling and simple leading that a foal is taught in the first weeks of its life, lungeing is the next logical step in its education. Most people like to lunge a horse a little at two years old before he becomes so strong that resistance is easy for him. At the end of a lungeing rein he learns the words of command you will later use when you back him at three years old. It builds the foundation of that responsive relationship between you. From the tone of your voice he learns whether he has executed the commands to halt, walk or trot correctly and he seems to enjoy the attention your voice signifies is being lavished on him.

More than that, it supples a horse to make him work on a circle. All horses have one stiff side which makes it difficult for them, when they are first ridden, to go forward in an absolutely straight line and makes them more liable to nap on one side rather than the other. By watching, you can see whether they work more easily on the left or the right and then concentrate on suppling the muscles belonging to the less elastic side.

Solomon was a nappy horse by temperament: chestnuts are frequently said to be 'hot' or wilful in this way. But the fault had been exacerbated by his loneliness, and by confusion too, as the clear, precise and sympathetic signals (or 'aids') that Liz had taught him came less exactly from my unpractised hand and leg. All these things together made him reluctant to enter into any working relationship with me.

I tried to see this impasse as a challenge, for it is also true that the best horses, the ones that go on to display boldness and brilliance, are those with a decided will and personality of their own. Often, they are the most intelligent of horses and if they can be matched by a rider of equal sensitivity and determination, they will gleam like the horses in my head had gleamed so many years before.

As Solomon's winter coat thickened and the days shortened, a new complication developed with problems for both of us.

My back is long because it has more than the usual number of component parts in it: every now and then one of them slides out in protest. I ignored the warning aches and twinges as long as I could. What I failed to realise was that my discomfort contributed directly to that of the horse.

A horse moving freely in the field can gallop, wheel extravagantly or stop without losing any of his grace or balance. The fluidity of his paces stems from a natural balancing of neck and quarters that keep his centre of gravity constant. Placing a human weight of some 140 lbs. on the back of a young horse, completely disrupts that relationship of parts and to help himself accommodate the new distribution of weight, the horse will lower his head and neck and allow his hind legs to straggle out behind him. The art of schooling a young horse is very slowly, very patiently, to re-create that former balance by building up the muscles of his neck and back and quarters until the lanky, somewhat clumsy outline of the young animal again becomes coiled and shortened. The neck becomes more shapely and arched, the head flexed, and as the quarters become more rounded, they are better able to power the horse's movement from behind, gradually restoring his natural spring. The horse's engine is at the rear. It is from here that all movements derive, here that the rider's control is directed. You don't stop a horse by pulling on its mouth. You don't turn him by tugging to left or right. Any decrease of pace is achieved by bracing your back down on his back to slow the impulsion of the quarters and you merely indicate that this is your intention by squeezing a restraining signal along the reins. You turn the horse by applying your left or right leg to shift his quarters and again, confirm your intention by squeezing gently on the relevant rein. The difference is critical. Understanding it, it is possible to see why small girls on riding-school ponies frequently appear to have no control at all. They imagine that all steering, stopping and starting is done at the head end and their ponies, desperate to escape the pain in their mouths, either stick their heads up in the air to evade the tugging or, mouths totally numbed by the action of the bit, they clamp their teeth against it, lower their heads and bolt for the horizon.

This brief account of a horse's dynamics is necessary to explain why my back was undermining what shreds of a relationship were left between Solomon and myself. Unconsciously, to save myself pain at the bottom of my spine, I was throwing my weight further and further forward with the result that the little horse was obliged to throw his weight further forward too. Head and neck drooped closer and closer to the ground, in which position his mouth was going 'dead'. He was virtually leaning on the bit and I was virtually holding his head up with my hands. I was completely destroying that lively, elastic contact between the rider's hand and the horse's mouth that is vital to any reading of the 'signals' between them.

I knew that something was seriously wrong. When Solomon wasn't making a sudden dash for home he carried me like a dying donkey. Needing expert help and too embarrassed to ask it of Liz, I sent Solomon to a schooling centre a few miles away at Trowbridge and creaking in every hinge, drove over there whenever I could for an evening's instruction in the covered school.

Part of the diagnosis was that he needed a 'schoolmaster', an older experienced horse who would give him both the companionship he lacked and confidence in his own learning.

It was a dismal conclusion and, for the moment, an impossibility, but I didn't come away from Trowbridge entirely empty handed. I returned with Solomon and an engaging, blond mongrel puppy.

4

"TAKE HIM," ANN, THE PROPRIETOR OF THE SCHOOL, HAD said. "He needs a good home."

The shaggy and entirely circular puppy was actively demonstrating his charm.

"What is he?"

"Half collie and half labrador – I think." She was rather vague about the movements of her bitch.

"What's he called?"

"Muffin."

"Oh, dear."

In the first place, Muffin is an extremely silly name (although it did rather become the round, yellow puppy). Secondly, I'd been fool enough to use it once before on an entirely unsuitable dog. Muffin One had been unsuitable in almost every respect. To begin with, he was a Corgi, not the kind of dog I normally care for at all. But more than that, to own a royal dog, to live in a robustly working-class area of London and to be forced to walk down the street at midnight, as late pub-leavers recover against the railings, calling out "Muffin! Mu-ffy!" at the top of your voice is to be the source of great and unwelcome merriment.

The dog was, anyway, insane having had its brain size reduced by overbreeding, I imagine. It ate only from the dustbin, drank only from the bathtap and, grasping that defecation was in some way associated with 'outside', would crap on the hall carpet before running smugly into the garden. Worst of all, it sexually assaulted the foot of any male visitor unwise enough to sit down and cross his legs in an inviting way.

"Muffin?" I repeated forlornly.

"Yes."

"Oh."

Muffin Two had leapt into the back of my car where he wriggled with pleasure. Looking at the very bright brown eyes that shone out of his chrysanthemum head, I felt appropriated.

Muffin retained his name since he answered to it. But the spherical shape that he'd had at six months lengthened into a predominantly Border collie shape. From the rear, that strain reveals itself in a plume of a tail and an assymetrical lope. His colouring, a pale, corn gold is all that remains of the labrador if that *is* what went into the mix.

He is the most satisfactory dog I have ever owned. He is all that a dog should be. One day he will die and I and my children will grieve dreadfully over him. For that reason I want them to have more than their own indifferent snapshots to remember him by.

They will want to remember him as a bounding, adoring presence who shared their games, who tried to follow them to school and, forcibly turned back, sat all day at the top of the hill waiting for them to return. A dog who defended

40

them against two reeling drunkards outside a pub one day, who ran beside their bicycles, tongue lolling, up and down the steep hills all the way to Batcombe and back, who chewed their school socks and survived more accidents than a nine-lived cat. He is the kind of dog, superficially nondescript with rather tangled blond wreaths of hair about his hind legs, who nonetheless moves strangers to stop and ask all about him while they fondle his kindly head. I think he is beautiful.

The dog I modelled on him in one of my novels I described as possessing perfect love. Muffin's love is so consuming it is a source of anguish to him at times. He feels it should be attached in equal quantities to every member of the family and if any two of us squabble or raise our voices in anger, he suffers terribly, darting protectively from one to the other, confused as to which has the greater claim on his loyalty. If I were ever to strike one of the children I am sure he would attack me. If John kisses me or holds me, even for a moment, he utters short, distraught barks that can, if we ignore him, acquire a faintly angry, upward snarl and then he wriggles his now rather large, ungainly body between our legs until content that some current of household love is passing through him too.

Most people are very clear in their preference when it comes to a general choice between cats and dogs. The unhesitating nature of their reply comes, I suspect, from the degree in which they feel their own personality is reflected in one or the other creature. Until the arrival of Muffin my preference was for cats and in the general sense, still is. But Muffin manages to stand outside generalisation.

I admire the independence of the cat, its relaxed contempt for the person who (laughably) describes himself as the owner of the creature. Nobody owns a cat. Its self-reliance is one of the absolutes of the world. I admire its litheness, its sureness of movement, its dangerous edge that makes it, even asleep on a fire-warmed rug, only a generation away from its bigger, more deadly relations.

By comparison dogs are coarse, and clumsy, and smelly,

41

and over-exuberant, and absurdly submissive, and always trying to catch your eye like an adolescent sweetheart. Only a lover would regard you as uncritically as the dog does. Or would start to his feet as you leave a room and plead to come with you however short the distance or boring the place you are going to. The cat in me despises that a little.

That is not what the dog-hater feels. The loathing of the dog-hater is a huge and irrational thing. His hatred is thick with repulsion for dirt. Diseases carried by dogs, dog faeces, dog hair, dog's fleas. I have walked with my dog along the beach and seen people scramble on hands and knees, brandishing their child's small spade as the dog amiably nears their dull sandcastles or heaps of clothing. Their eyes bulge with hate.

I remember parking below Hardy's monument in Dorset (Kiss-me Hardy not Thomas Hardy), where the gorse-covered heathland pours down towards a green sea and the weird pebble shelf of Chesil Beach and there, as I lifted the picnic things out of the boot of my car, I became aware of a face framed within the window of a nearby car. It was a red face, heavily jowled, flattened at the top by a white peak cap. Its owner's eyes, pale with anger, were fixed on the rear wheel of his new white car where Muffin stood on three legs.

"Your dog," said the man in the cap, scarcely able to get the words out. "Your dog has just peed on my car. Get him away! Get off! Put him on the lead!"

"Oh, deary, deary me," I said and whistled the dog.

"He *peed* on my car!"

He seemed to need soothing. "I shouldn't get so over-excited about it if I were you," I suggested. A slow implosion took place inside his head while his wife in the passenger seat turned *her* head away from the danger zone and regarded the view through the other window.

"He *peed* on my car!" the man repeated as if I couldn't have heard him the first time. "How would you like it if I came and peed on your car?"

"Feel free," I said. "Any time."

Truly, I thought he was going to fragment into small red,

42

jagged pieces of himself. It must be a terrible thing to hate dogs so deeply. Life must be fraught with hazard and fury, no excursion safe to undertake.

A friend of mine who is a most warm and affectionate mother and considers cats sacred, lets her children hit my dog on his head with their toys and doesn't even appear to notice. It's a very odd thing, this division of taste. *My* preference for cats doesn't prohibit feeling for dogs at all. Certainly not for Muffin who took it upon himself, during the unexpectedly long period of nearly four years John was obliged to work away from home, to guard me and be, of all the animals I accumulated round me as companions in that time, the most constantly attendant. Before Muffin arrived I often used to lie awake straining to distinguish suspicious sounds from the conversation of owls and the rasping gargle of the vixen as the great width of night descended between me and my neighbours. I kept a shotgun by my bed and my tennis shoes underneath it, in case I ever needed to make a quick getaway. With Muffin roaming round the house at night I fear nothing.

His most redeeming feature in those early days was the unusual independence (some might call is disobedience) he displayed. Like Frank Harris, he had a secret life, except that it was not so very secret. It amounted to a public nuisance.

At the bottom of our steep south-facing slope the road winds westward to Wyke Champflower. Facing us on the far side of it is the northerly slope of our neighbours' gardens. Their cabbages and bean rows and life in general are (like ours) exposed to view. There are incalculable benefits to this topography. Because the tree tops are below you, the birds fly at eye-level. And in the lush months of May or June when the trees are heavy with leaf and the grass is as deep and full of movement as the sea, it seems, when you are standing watching visitors depart, as if they are stepping down into green water.

The disadvantages are that you can be seen, whatever you do. Equally, that Muffin, sitting at the top of the hill and maturing fast, could see not only the bitches belonging to our immediately facing neighbours, the Walkers, but worse, those dogs a hundred yards further west along the valley that were in the care of Jack Hopkins, the kennel owner.

Often I would look up from what I was doing and see a jubilant blond shape in pursuit of the Walkers' Dalmatian or stalking a whole collection of agreeable bitches being exercised across the hill by Jack. Or I would simply hear the scream of brakes and a prolonged hooting in the road below. It was no good. As soon as Muffin thought my attention was secured by something else, his characteristic lopsided rear could be glimpsed stealing off down the hill.

At first I supposed obedience training would be enough to overcome the problem. Jack, who considered him a thoroughly badly controlled dog, held classes which Muffin and I attended.

He was the star of the class. Heel, walk on, sit, stay, no matter what the order, Muffin's collie instinct responded instantly. While other owners disentangled themselves from knotted leads and became slightly violet in the face as their commands were ignored, Muffin lay quietly at my feet watching his classmates with disapproval. Jack was astonished, a little incredulous to be truthful, to see Muffin behaving with irreproachable meekness.

He would walk to heel all the way along the road home and then, the moment he thought my attention was deflected, slink quietly off for a more interesting session at Jack Hopkins' kennels.

Not until he was eighteen months old, the November after I'd first brought him home, was I persuaded that the only way to cope with the problem was castration. By that time he'd been run over twice and my neighbours' patience was understandably wearing thin. Great as the nuisance was to them, my greater fear was that he would cause a road accident and somebody might be terribly injured.

I delivered him to the vet one morning before going on to the BBC at Bristol to talk to Johnny Morris on Woman's Hour about people and their animals. I felt despicable.

When I called back that night, he hadn't come round from

the anaesthetic. By morning he was still out cold and I was growing anxious. At first, when I called again in the evening, the vet was dubious about his going, but Muffin, hearing my voice, recovered in an instant. However he was still very dopey when we arrived home in the dark. He fell out of the car, staggered off into the night and disappeared. I searched and searched. He was finally discovered across the road sniffing wistfully about the Walkers' garden.

"It takes a little while," the vet said over the phone. "His hormones are still circulating."

It took a week.

After that, Muffin sat at the top of the hill in his customary place, gazing across at the Walkers' bitches bounding among the fruit trees, his nose pointing to an indefinable scent, his features bearing a puzzled expression.

He still wanders a little, usually in pursuit of me. More than once, some distance from home, I have seen – looking in my rear view mirror – a pale gold shape, tongue drooping like a pink rag, lolloping down the centre of the road behind me.

Not everyone loves Muffin unreservedly.

In spite of a nature so gentle that he will allow my small nieces to tread all over him, hauling themselves up on fistfuls of his curling hair, he is a good house dog. That is a fine way of saying he frightens a lot of perfectly innocent people out of their wits.

It all began with the newspaper boy who must, without any ill-intention, have raised his rolled newspaper at him one day. Since then, Muffin's special wrath – and it is a fearsome, snarling performance, lips rolled back from apparently twice the number of teeth any normal dog should have – has been kept for callers carrying something in their hand. This makes life unnecessarily exciting for our very tolerant postmen, deliverers of the parish magazine, collectors for Christian Aid and a remarkably large number of men who call at a certain season of the year saying they've recently

45

come into possession of a quantity of tarmac which could usefully and reasonably, be rolled on our drive.

Nowadays I don't try and prevent the dog hurtling downhill barking and growling as though desperate for human flesh. He takes no notice. Indeed, the more I call, the more he seems to interpret my voice as a defenceless woman's cry for help. But I did, initially, try to build some sort of friendship between Keith, the newspaper boy, and Muff.

Keith had refused to deliver any more newspapers so I hung about, waiting for him in the dark early mornings in an effort to persuade him that the dog was harmless.

A woman who jumps out from behind a gate in the pitch dark proved to be every bit as alarming as a ferocious dog. Keith retreated from me as fast as he decently could without actually running.

"He's all bark and no bite," I called through the gloom, hurrying after him. "Honestly."

"I'm not going near that dog!" Keith kept walking.

"Truly, he's very gentle."

"I'm not coming near him!" His voice came back through the dim atmosphere.

I tried on other mornings, not helped by Muffin's cannoning downhill, throat unattractively exposed. Then John tried intercepting Keith. The experience was becoming too much for the boy. The entire family as well as the dog was clearly off its head. His protests became more agitated. "That dog," he shouted as he hurried away in the pre-dawn darkness, "came to our house and attacked my mother."

We let the matter drop. I don't blame Keith. Muffin can look uncommonly unpleasant when he tries.

Some months later John met Keith walking down Providence Place with a small black and white dog on a lead.

"Hello Keith," cried John, attempting to be friendly. "I didn't know you had a dog. *Isn't* he nice!" And he bent down to pat the animal. It bit him.

5

WE HAD COME TO KNOW THE HOLGATES WELL. THEY were kind, generous and idiosyncratic in equally abundant proportion. They fed us handsomely, on occasions advised us on everything from re-seeding to shoeing and lent us any tool or piece of equipment we both needed and lacked. Like most country people, if asked for help, they gave as if giving were one of life's greatest delights.

Some three months after buying Solomon, Liz rang me. She was going north to see a dealer from whom she occasionally bought horses. He had a grey mare she wanted to look at. "She sounds just right for you," Liz said. "How can you possibly know?" I wondered, feeling far from able to buy a second horse although I had been working rather hard with that unformed aim fluttering in the back of my mind.

"I dreamt about her last night." Liz sounded convinced.

Liz says she is a witch. She isn't really, though there's a deal of Irish blood in her. It's Hugh in fact, by no means a natural psychic, who claims to have been surprised one day by seeing all his dead relatives conversing happily in the woodland – surprised, less by seeing them than by seeing them converse *happily* together. But that's by the by. On the phone, Liz reiterated her conviction.

She was even more certain after seeing the mare.

"She's *just* what you need!"

"I don't actually *need* anything."

"She's up to plenty of weight – could carry John – wonderfully schooled and a good jumper." I was still pondering the weight-carrying properties of the mare as Liz pressed on. "She used to be a showjumper but got sick of it and began to stop so she's going quite cheap . . ." That sounded much less promising. "She's bound to jump all right out hunting . . ."

"Just a moment . . ."

". . . And she has a thoroughly nice, honest expression," Liz steamed on.

Her insistence was in the end effective. As soon as we could find a day, John and I drove north to Cheshire.

I wish I could say the dealer had a nice, honest expression. Hair neatly oiled, wearing twill trousers, an expensive shortie coat and suede shoes, he was certainly the master of an impeccable-looking yard. He was vaguely familiar to me as the kind of man I'd known in my youth: the father of the only small girls with decent ponies.

He had two horses for me to look at. "We *are* only looking," I emphasised peering up from my curiously bent position. A long drive in the car had me locked in a gargoyle shape. It was rather difficult to lever me on to a horse at all.

The first horse, a hot, breedy kind was too good and too expensive. The grey mare, absurdly but flawlessly plaited to impress the potential customer, was slow, steady and for somebody with a slipped disc, wonderfully comfortable. It was like riding a large sofa.

"Thank you for letting us *look!*" I acknowledged, lowering myself gingerly back into the car. "Very nice."

"A bit dull, I thought," said John as we drove off. John, who had also tried her, has ridden unshod Arab ponies up cliff faces in the Cameroons and is rather contemptuous of anything quiet. "On the other hand," he observed thoughtfully, "she *is* just right for you in a sense. She looks just like you."

"What?"

"She has quite a nice face, a very long back and very short legs."

"Thanks a lot," I moaned through gritted teeth.

I thought about it. I even arranged for a vet to look her over. The vet, an Irishman with a voice that sounded as though Guinness lapped his epiglottis, rang me to say the mare was in the most perfect health and about eight years old.

"*Eight?*" I echoed disbelievingly.

"Well, maybe nine. Not a month more. A lovely mare if I may say so."

It was December. Approaching Christmas. A present from me to me.

Liz rang. "She'd be ideal for you to hunt."

"I'm not . . ."

I rang the dealer back, got fifty pounds off and free delivery. "I'll bring the vet's certificate with me," he promised and we made mutually satisfied noises at either end of the phone.

A few days later he appeared leading my mare up the hill.

"What's the matter with her face?" I asked. She had a very beautiful face and large, expressively dark eyes.

"Face?" He looked earnestly in the fading light. "Ah. That's where the halter's rubbed her in the box, I expect. Long journey. Longer than I *expected*." He said it as though I'd robbed him.

I peered more closely at the small raw patches as the dealer's wife materialised and toiled up the hill behind us. She was small and plump with dyed yellow hair and wore a

49

tight-fitting trouser suit. "Bloody 'ell," she puffed. She gave the impression of a woman in need of drink.

I took the mare, trying not to look too anxiously at the sore areas of her face. "Did you bring the vet's certificate?"

"Damn me!" Husband and wife gazed at one another as if the other could not be relied upon to remember anything at all. "I'll post it on," said the wife, dabbing at her forehead with a little hanky. "Steep drive you've got." Her make-up was cracking.

The next day the sore spots were worse and the mare was indefinably uneasy. Whether unwell or unsettled by the journey I couldn't tell, but when John tied her up to examine her more closely she ran back in a panic, breaking the rope. Reluctant to be patted or soothed she flinched away from our attentions, circling the box and thrusting her head over the door to blow suspiciously at the strange air. Solomon, leaning over his door, nearly fell out of his stable with excitement. I put him out in the paddock first and he stood by the gate, waiting, making himself look terribly well bred as he tossed his head and flared his nostrils. When I drew near the narrow gate with the grey mare, she made a sudden, hysterical plunge through it, knocking me to the ground and galloping over me.

"I'm so *pleased* you've got her!" It was Liz on the phone. "Aren't you *pleased*?"

Obviously I sounded less enthralled than I should.

"Can I come over and see her soon? She's such a lovely mare!"

I wanted the vet to come over and see her first. I rang him.

"Two things. I think she has ringworm and I'm not sure she's sound."

The round, hairless spots on her face were beginning to appear on her body. Ringworm is highly contagious. Already, I'd started disinfecting bedding and rugs. The vet wasn't sure she had ringworm, but she certainly had something. Like all good vets and doctors, he had a suitable ointment.

Next, I trotted her out for him.

50

"Once more," he said thoughtfully, watching her legs for any oddity of gait.

Leading her, we trotted together. I was far more notice-ably unsound than the mare. As I hopped up and down, she must have looked perfect by contrast. "I think it's just her action," the vet concluded. "She tends to rock from side to side quite naturally."

She did have a curious action, throwing her feet out side-ways as she trotted. That's what had made her seem so com-fortable.

"She's a nice, useful sort of mare." The vet looked her over approvingly.

"How old would you say she is?" I ventured.

He thrust a thumb in one corner of her mouth and rolled back the upper lip to study her teeth. "About . . . twelve?"

I rang the vet in Cheshire.

"Do you have ringworm in your area?"

"Funny you should say that. I saw a case only today. No, don't tell me . . . Oh deary me!"

"I haven't had a certificate yet."

'Not had a certificate? Now, wasn't Gordon going to bring it with him?"

"He was."

"And you've not got it! Deary me, now. Shall I be posting you a copy?"

"If you would," I said coldly.

I never did receive a vet's certificate for Bathsheba.

Perhaps I would have pressed further with it had I not been busy preparing Christmas for ten people and spending an inconvenient amount of time on an electrically heated plate and, subsequently, the couch of a chiropractor who finally and honestly declared he could do nothing for me. I survived Christmas on pain-killers, gin and very little sleep, only too glad to fall out of bed at five in the morning and muck out by torchlight. There is no better restorative in the world than watching dawn crack across a black winter's sky. A

51

thin slice of gold opens up in the east and fills with fire. The first shape to emerge is the dovecote on its lonely little hill.

In the belief that a hard, unexpected blow would push back whatever had fallen out, I continued to ride. The theory didn't work as planned. Sitting astride Bathsheba bareback one morning, transfixed by the unexpectedly sharp rocks of her spine which threatened to saw me clean through from bottom to top if she made a move, I fell off like a stone when Matthew opened the back door and made her shy. I was banged about in an ambulance to Bath where a workmanlike sculptress stripped me, bandaged me from armpit to thigh and then, while I tried to stand upright, slapped layers of icy plaster on top. It was very damp but marvellously comfortable in there. Something else was holding me up. The only drawback was, I didn't bend.

A builder friend lent me a pair of steps. Climbing these, while persuading Bathsheba to stand still alongside, I was able to lie over the saddle and then, by some graceless manoeuvre, to lie full length, face down along her back, shuffling myself forward into the saddle. I had to sit very straight and move very slowly, otherwise the plaster cast pinched my bottom unmercifully.

On New Year's Day I was taken to hospital and there I remained for the next two months.

This is not the place for hospital reminiscences. All I shall say for now is that I was immensely relieved to be removed from the first hospital, where a spasmodically raving woman died of neglect in the bed next to me and was then removed from her plaster cast by a power drill which ground through a ward stilled by shock.

At the second hospital which was crowded and kindly, it was discovered that I, too, had been a little neglected. They gave me a very thorough blanket bath and fixed additional traction to my toes which had been allowed to droop, thus shortening the back tendons in my leg. Finally it was decided that an operation was the only means of removing the literally intractable disc.

News of the operation was received with muted gloom not only by friends, who had heard nothing good of it and implied from their expressions that I would never ride again, but also by a fellow patient called Fanny who was recovering from a hip operation. Delighted by her new hip, she came to show me her legs every day. At seventy-six Fanny had a spindly pair of shanks but she was glad to dance on them. "You *do* remind me of Ann," she mused every time she passed. "She was in this bed before you. *She* had your operation. She had it twice. It went wrong the first time. You *do* remind me of Ann." I reminded her of Ann on at least four separate occasions every day, but since I was suspended head down from ropes and pulleys, there was no escaping Fanny's friendly attentions.

There was also ample time to worry about my family. The two sets of grandparents, who had packed their cases and waved goodbye after Christmas, returned in shifts rather sooner than they'd planned and took over. John, who was working in London, drove to Bath so often he was almost beyond speech as he sat beside my bed, weariness deepening every line of his face. Everything was fine, he murmured.

And really it was. We were very lucky. The children were far cleaner and better cared for than usual. Their socks were darned, not a button was missing from their shirts. The bottoms of my saucepans were scrubbed and all the plants were watered.

Twice every day Jack Hopkins came over to do the horses, bringing them in at night down the dark hillside and mucking out at dawn with a practised speed and elegance that exceeded anything I could do.

I was determined that I should ride again. The prolonged rest, I argued to myself as the old ladies snored and whimpered through the lengthy nights, was just what Solomon needed. He could be left to grow and strengthen and together we would start his education again in the spring.

But it was Hugh who stopped the sidelong disappointment that sometimes sneaked into my imagination. (Perhaps, I thought, as the lead weights gently whined, perhaps I was never intended to ride a real horse. Perhaps fate was preserving me from far worse accidents. Perhaps . . .) Hugh came bearing a jar of pickled onions with a plastic fork secured to its neck by a length of baler twine. Hugh and I keep up a running quality check on pickled onions. It is the crispness that counts. (John now does an excellent pickled onion: hot, so spicy it can take your head clean off your shoulders. He's mastered the crispness problem. The secret is to steep your onions in cold not, as the recipe books recommend, hot vinegar.)

"I thought you'd probably be needing these," Hugh bellowed.

The ward sister scurried to him like a nun and told him to keep his voice down. For a few moments, he genuinely tried.

"You ought to get that mare of yours in foal," he urged in a substantial whisper. "As soon as you get out of here we'll go and take a look at some likely stallions."

Other people's nearby visitors remained crouched and silent, their interest caught like kites in the wind.

"I've got just the stallion for you in mind," he declared.

"Sh-sh-sh!" The anorexic sister bore down on him hissing, finger to her lips.

A foal. As they bore me off to remove the offending disc, I fixed my mind on the possibility.

One shining February morning my father-in-law came to fetch me home. I had something resembling a section of the Great Western Railway stitched from rear end to waist and was rigidly contained in a steel corset. Snow glistened on the smooth, unspoilt white hills that spread round Bath. The sky rose, a huge unblemished dome of blue. The air smelt clean. At home, snowdrops pressed through the snow, the green of their leaves a brave and tender colour.

When Matthew saw me walk again he burst into tears.

54

For two months he had silently lodged in his heart the belief that he had caused the fall which led to my going away. He showed me all the drawings he'd done in my absence. It was lovely to be back.

6

WINTER JASMINE, SMALL, WAXY ACONITES, FORSYTHIA and daffodils blazed yellow against the wintry bareness of the March hedgerows. I was supposed to spend three month inside the steel corset. I was supposed to swim.

So was Hugh, who had also suffered back injuries when his own horse had been killed under him by a speeding, sun-blinded car a year before. Dutifully, we took our rolled up towels to Yeovil swimming pool and sat in the café opposite abandoning the idea.

"There's a splendid stud near Trowbridge," he said.

Bathsheba perplexed me. Unlike Solomon who, for all his opposition under the saddle, whinnied joyously every time he saw me and came readily to be caught, Bathsheba wouldn't allow herself to be known. She remained silent and withdrawn. Jack Hopkins told me that she'd pursued him round the stable for twenty minutes, refusing to let him out on the first occasion he took a hay net to her. She was unwilling to be caught in the field and came only once Solomon was lead ahead of her. Then she would trail after us, some ten suspicious yards behind.

She had an unexplained quality, something that moved me. Her sweet and gentle expression betrayed hurt but what had gone into the making of that hurt I couldn't tell. She still bounded through gateways with evident fear though I was now wise enough to stand aside at a safe distance. She still tried to run back on her powerful haunches when tied up. Whether she'd been injured at a gate either jumping it or being crowded and kicked by other horses, whether she'd been tied up in a box and soundly beaten by an ill-tempered rider after a bad round in the ring, I could only wonder about. Towards me she showed a resigned tolerance, letting me catch and handle her without protest but with a guardedness I was unable to dispel.

I couldn't have ridden her more than half a dozen times since I'd had her and then only very undemandingly. On those few occasions she'd remained dully obedient as if soured by experience though too well-mannered to behave with open resentment.

"She's older than twelve, that mare," Jack Hopkins declared. "Just look how white her coat has become. She's too wise. She knows too much. Nearer fifteen or sixteen, I'd say." And then, with a thoughtful draw on his pipe, "Maybe more."

Mr. Godden showed us round his yard. There were heavy-bellied brood mares close to foaling, a few youngsters he had bred himself to sell on and three fine stallions fit and ready for their season's service.

Hugh stood in the centre of the yard, hair escaping under his cap, legs precariously bearing up his height and waved the stallions round him one by one. Each was led in turn by

57

the stud groom whose feet, every now and then, left the ground as one of the powerful animals tossed its head fightingly high in the air.

"Watch out!" warned Hugh, staggering away from a flying hind leg. "You know what to look for?" he yelled as I hung back against the wall thinking that all stallions without exception looked crazy.

"Bone!" he roared, in answer to his own question and pointed his stick at the animal's legs. "Plenty of bone!"

Bone, I had thankfully learned somewhere, indicated the dimension of the cannon bone which runs from knee or hock to the fetlock joint. This is the area that has to sustain most strain in the ridden horse and an animal with too little substance is liable to go lame very easily. Ideally, it should be short and straight and strong, about eight to nine inches round. Too thick a leg merely denotes commonness. I studied bone.

"And a good outlook . . ." The stick waved at the horse's head.

"A good, sloping shoulder . . ."

"A nicely let-down pair of hocks . . ."

"A good eye . . ."

"A free mover . . ."

"Most of all . . . a kind temperament."

I stared earnestly. None of the stallions possessed an evidently kind temperament. One of them, a gleaming black animal standing seventeen three hands high, was trying to eat the groom. Mentally, I crossed it off my list.

"This is the one!"

An immediate leap of agreement flew through me.

Master Spiritus stood seventeen hands high. An ex-steeplechaser, he was a fine glowing bay with yellow-toned highlights in his coat. He was the only one who led sweetly.

"Thoroughly good temperament," said Hugh.

And so it was arranged that when Bathsheba next came into season, she should be brought to be covered by this magnificent animal.

"Should breed a perfect hunting type," commented Hugh.

58

Two weeks later she was loaded into a borrowed trailer and taken to stud.

John came too. I wanted him to see Master Spiritus who was behind bars in a roomy box. A large and ugly wound gaped open on his backside.

"What on earth has happened?" I asked Mr. Godden.

"Oh, 'tis nothing." Mr. Godden, who has a voice as brown and rounded as a nut, smiled. "If he doesn't have a mare before breakfast he gets a bit angry and bites hisself."

It seemed an extreme way of showing frustration. I wondered anew about the kindness of his temperament and worried about Bathsheba.

"He'll be right as ninepence in a minute," Mr. Godden soothed. "We'll have your mare served this afternoon."

I hoped that Master Spiritus would have at least two mares for lunch and left with some apprehension.

A mare comes into season once every three weeks between (roughly) December and June. She carries her foal for a full year. Racehorse owners like to breed their stock early – in January or February – and don't mind facing the expense of keeping a horse in and feeding it hay and corn because they have well-grown stock ready for two-year-old races. (I have to confess that racing animals at two years, when their bones are still so green that they often break down by four, seems to me far more cruel than steeplechasing). The ordinary breeder prefers to have his mare foal in the spring when the new grass is growing and the animals can be turned out to mature naturally. It was now early April. Without design, I seemed to have timed things rather well.

"She hasn't taken," Mr. Godden informed me over the phone. "She's come into season again." It meant a further three weeks at stud and what had begun as an exciting venture (stud fee: £35) was beginning to become an expensive and possibly fruitless undertaking: a common pattern of affairs if you keep horses, as I was rapidly beginning to learn. Indeed, half the purpose of producing a good foal was to recoup some

59

of my losses. (Apart from anything else, I hadn't been fit enough to work properly for nearly six months and there's no sick pay for freelancers.)

Three more weeks passed.

"She seems to have a slack womb," reported Mr. Godden on the phone. A slack womb sounded serious. "If you're agreeable, the vet suggests a hormone implant."

I was far too involved by now to withdraw. A hormone implant meant sewing a small pellet into Bathsheba's neck which would release regular quantities of oestrogen into the bloodstream and thus, apparently, tighten the womb. Without it she might abort. The pellet would somehow have to be found and removed a month before foaling was due, but that was a problem I was prepared to leave aside for nearly a year.

"Fine," I responded limply and sat down to write as many articles as one can at a single sitting in a steel corset.

As the shining future propect of a foal began to dim a little the resolve to ride renewed itself. My three months probation weren't quite up but I couldn't see the harm in it. Solomon was saddled for a short walk around the fields. Nothing more than that. Muffin ran alongside, tail wagging, darting off now and then in uncommitted pursuit of baby rabbits whose white scuts vanished into the bramble patches like blown dandelion clocks.

It felt very odd. My muscles resembled limp fillets lying on a butcher's slab. But it was good to be out in the long valley meadow with the chestnut trees that step up the gentle hillsides coming into fulsome leaf.

As we turned for home Solomon too, was flooded with joy. The short grass turning a vivid green beneath him made him buck once, then twice before galloping headlong down the springy hollow of turf.

I fell flat on my back. For a moment I lay there wondering if I dare move. I tried. I held. I was all right.

I was all right! The fact that I'd torn a ligament in my right hand was beside the point. The glue had worked. The vertebrae, fused together at the bottom of my spine, were

60

still stuck together. Using my left hand, I tapped out a note to the surgeon and told him what a splendid job he'd done.

My writing hand bound up, I went to collect Bathsheba who appeared to have 'held'. A very hot-faced groom handed her over to me. "Do you ever have any trouble catching this mare?" he enquired.

"Not really. Only if a man tries to catch her."

"Well, four men have just spent two hours trying to catch her. She's a funny one, that mare."

7

APPLE BLOSSOM LAY ACROSS THE LITTLE CIDER ORCHARDS like a wedding canopy. In the hedgerows, flowering hawthorn was succeeded by creaming cups of elder and the fields deepened with purple clover, dandelions, buttercups and a sudden flush of towering red fescue.

The sweep of growth in May as the soil warms is heartening and, if you live in the country, exhausting. There is planting, last-minute digging and much cutting back to be done. Docks and nettles double their size overnight. Cow parsley foams waist high under the trees. As the evenings lighten, the work increases with the day's own length and by the end of the month, the farmers trail homewards on tractors towing loads of grass cuts for silage in the low, sinking light of a sun that sets after nine o'clock.

Even for us the labour expanded. The more we worked, the more we learned. In this, the Holgates played their unfailingly generous part. Liz attempted to teach me that lungeing is pointless if you don't stand relatively firm in the centre of your circle. Wandering after the horse on his own chosen circuit profits neither of you. Indeed, Solomon perceiving the ease with which I could be drawn after him, dragged me the full length of the paddock and tore another ligament in another finger of my right hand.

In the meantime, our re-seeded grass was growing and with two horses to keep, needed to be fenced off fairly urgently. Hugh had sighed over the spectacle of John solemnly digging each post hole the previous summer. "My dear chap . . ." he had murmured, eyes raised despairingly. Next time, he promised, he would come over with his tractor and its special post-holer digger attachment. He did.

Hugh had not allowed for the acute angle of the hill. The alignment of the post-hole digger was such that given our gradient, it could do no more than scratch the surface of the earth. Hugh dismounted the tractor, scratched his head, blasphemed generally about the inadequacies of modern technology, secured his trousers more firmly with baler twine and began digging post holes by hand. It took him a week.

A farmer who finds much to lament in modern agriculture – not least the number of forms that require to be filled – Hugh still cannot resist planning projects on his land. He is descended from Capability Brown and certain inherited genes, I suspect, account for a number of these projects. The erection of a gazebo, for example. The building of an Irish bank in his front garden for horses to jump over which, in turn, led to the building of an entire cross-country course over the fields. Sometimes the projects are less ambitious but all are ardently undertaken, none more so than the creation of a perfect eco-system pond in the garden. It was one of those things you send away for. Not a large pond, but one carefully supplied with all the correct plants, newts, tiddlers and so forth. The water for this small pond had to be transported from elsewhere if things were to thrive in it. All was

63

completed and I called to admire the finished creation. As I stood indoors with Liz chatting and gazing out of the window at this lovingly made object, Muffin leapt out of the Land Rover, pursued one of the Holgates' fourteen cats across the lawn, landed in the pond and distributed newts, weeds and lilies in every direction. The pond was emptied of its very particular water. I mention this only to demonstrate how great and resilient the friendship of the Holgates has been.

It was Hugh, for instance, who taught me how to milk. Not a cow, but a goat. Hugh has little time for cows although he allows other people's to graze his fields and break his fences. Economically, temperamentally – in every conceivable way – he is convinced of the goat's superiority. Both he and Liz were insistent that we should keep them, and so persuasive was their combined praise of the goat it seemed only sensible, that as soon as a kid was available, I should have one. But first I thought it wise to learn how to milk the creature.

It is very evident if you visit the goat tent at the great Royal Bath and West Show (our major local event) that people who keep goats are mad. They are quite unlike other stockbreeders, perhaps because the unique nature of the goat requires a very specific human to appreciate and understand it. You are either for or against the goat. Passionately. Both sides have the strongest possible arguments for their case and will launch into them with a wild, assertive intensity whenever the opportunity arises.

I had not, at that stage in my life, been exposed to the anti-goat lobby. I knew nothing of the objections. Later, the division over goats, reproduced in our own home, was to come nearer to breaking up our marriage than anything else before or since.

All that I then absorbed from the Holgates was that a goat yields proportionately more milk per acre than a cow, its gestation period is shorter, it has two teats rather than four, which gives less margin for infection, it will eat all manner of rubbish a cow will spurn, the milk itself is creamier, freer from impurities and extremely good for weak digestions, ulcers, asthma, eczema and weaning infants of all sorts.

"Right," said Hugh, bearing a bucket that looked absurdly small in his large hand. He tied up the white goat and gave it a few oats, then lowered himself with some difficulty into the not perfectly clean straw. A goat's udder is considerably lower than that of a cow. Unless you raise the entire goat to a reasonable level you have no choice but to lower yourself to its level. A stool is useless. So you sit on the straw with your legs stretched out.

Hugh seized the two teats with his hands showing me how to close off the supply of milk between thumb and forefinger, then stroking the trapped quantity of milk out with the remaining fingers. You do not squeeze with the entire hand. You do not allow the milk to shoot back upwards into the udder. Either movement will make the goat leap in protest. It is a task far more easily performed by a woman because her hands are smaller. The shorter your fingers the more sympathetic a milker you are likely to be. I am blessed with perfect milking hands. Nobody will ever ask me to do a commercial for nail varnish but there are advantages to owning a pair of strong, square hands with untapered nails. I acquitted myself well. The goat didn't hold up on me (if they don't care for you they can somehow retain the milk in the udder) and my wrists didn't ache as I'd been warned they would.

Hugh then demonstrated the final stage with his work-thickened fingers: stripping off.

"You must always strip off completely," he explained to my initial astonishment.

Firmly, he ran a forefinger and thumb down each emptied teat. "If you don't get the last drop out, you have mastitis to deal with."

He performed another wringing movement. The goat stepped into the bucket, raised her tail, let forth a shower of pellets into the milk and continued eating peaceably.

"Ah well," pronounced Hugh after a brief pause. He plunged a hand into the milk and fished around for the pellets. "What the eye doesn't see the heart doesn't grieve for."

And, with grand gesture, he flung out whatever he was able to recover.

Although the Holgates have been our principal helpers, advisers and teachers, we owe a debt to many others. Mr. Walker lends us one of his rotavators whenever we need one and then stands in his garden on the opposite slope watching it fall to pieces in John's hands. Once, without a word of reproach he came over himself after seeing three separate rotavators disintegrate, and rotavated the entire vegetable patch himself, refusing to stop until the light vanished at ten o'clock. And there's Jack Hopkins who has rescued me from trouble many a time, Joss Edwin who patiently returns our animals from his herd and has helped us cut hay, Ken Parfitt who smilingly comes to retrieve his cows from our paddocks and makes good the damage by lending us anything we care to ask for and Eddie Taylor, our nearest neighbouring farmer who, that first full summer, cut our tiny crop of silky, re-seeded grass. It was a dangerous manoeuvre to perform in a small area on so steep a slope and difficult to work out the looping pattern of cutting that prevents a farmer disturbing grass already cut or giving himself impossibly tight turns to perform. Eddie nearly turned himself and his tractor upside down into Providence Place but somehow he survived the curve on two wheels.

The whole essence of country life is contained in haymaking. Even without a bent line of scythers moving down the length of a field, even without stooks or hay stacks to be seen, it remains a central ritual of the working year. Throughout June the grass is anxiously watched for growth and then, when the moment between flowering and seeding comes and the hay is at its sweetest and best, the gaze turns just as anxiously to the sky for, to be perfect, the sun must shine without break for a week on the cutting, the drying, the turning and baling that is to be done.

Before the dew is dried off the morning grass, work starts. Grass that is slightly wet cuts more easily. At four, the tractors are out. It is always a gamble. Everything the farmer does is a risk. Some cut early in the year because the weather is fine and even if the yield is low the quality will be so good that their beasts will thrive on it in the winter months. Others delay, hoping for quantity, fearful of having to buy in more hay at inflated prices if there's a long, cold, wet spring next year and the animals can't be turned out but have to stand blaring and poorly conditioned in a slurry-filled yard.

Haymaking can stretch over June, July and August. After the wet, malevolent summer of 1974 I saw hay being made in October but generally there seems to be a mutually agreed fortnight when the valleys are filled with the steady buzz of tractors and the fields are striped with pale, bluish green ropes of cut grass. The fragrance of escaped and drying juices is everywhere and when the neat green parcels are stacked away, their sweetness acquires a warmth which has to be cautiously sniffed. Should the bales be a little too damp, the arrangement of them a little too close, that summer scent, the crushing of herbs that takes anxiety out of the winter months ahead, can become a threatening, treacly odour and you know some of your crop is lost: blackened and mouldy.

After the hay as been taken the patchwork of the country has more yellow squares worked into it. With a little rain it will green again and the animals can be moved on to the new, resilient pasture.

The first hay we ever took, forty-three bales, nearly a ton in all – off only one half of an acre – was a source of great pride and delight to me, not merely of the romantic kind. It represented fifty pounds worth of winter feed for my horses. As the bales stood, up-ended against one another to dry, it began to rain. To the bewilderment and, doubtless, the hilarity, of my neighbours, I ran and draped them with every possible piece of plastic covering. It was a totally misplaced protective impulse since they steamed away in a surly fashion under their plastic and I lost a good number. I know more about haymaking now.

Although the little scale and nature of my experiences can justifiably be thought of as pure self-indulgence, they've

67

helped me understand more keenly the way anxiety and insecurity are part of the weave of a farmer's existence. And I wonder sometimes how it is those men in Brussels can slide green pounds and paper subsidies across the top of an office table without once looking outside at the shape of the clouds that can make such a comedy of their careful scheming.

8

S LOWLY, SOLOMON SEEMED MORE AMENABLE.
I rode him early before the flies could trouble him,
before the sounds of milking even. (From six the swish-
ing and clanking starts up from half a dozen dairy farms
scattered within a half mile radius ... the ring of metal, then
a humming, an occasional oath, faint but clear.) We were out
before that, at the nocturnal creatures' brightest hour.

One sparkling summer morning we emerged from the
sunken part of Huish Lane, a narrow, rutted track overhung
by hazel and elder to see, through the thin, gold mist still
wreathing the hillside, a large red dog fox. He stared at us
steadily, then loped a little way ahead of us without any
quickening of pace into a high, bramble-covered bank that
contains the badger kingdom.

Their setts, hundreds of years old, maze the hill for a quarter of a mile. They say the badger is a disappearing species. Not in Somerset where their summer tracks flatten the tall dewy grass and show up as thin bare paths in the winter. I cannot count the times a fine striped head has made its sudden black and white appearance in the headlights of a car at night. Often, they will run ahead of the light, usually lolloping safely into the general greyness, but it's not at all uncommon to see the large dead body of a badger cast up against the verge next morning. They do say badger feasts are still celebrated hereabouts. Certainly I know of one person with badger ham in their deep freeze.

By June, Bathsheba was growing fat and lethargic; a combination of pregnancy and summer grass. We acquired our first hens and a new white kitten.

I gave Blot to Matthew for his birthday. A pretty creature, as small and neat as a porcelain ornament, she proved to be a rather boring cat. Tiger's disapproval of her was so pronounced he left home for a fortnight, returning lean and crusted round the ears with microscopic rabbit fleas. Through a magnifying glass they look like moving caviare.

Aurora ruffled her long tawny hair until satisfied she was twice her natural size and spat. However justified by Blot's sheer dullness, their inhospitable behaviour was such that Muffin seemed to feel a courteous need to befriend the small white kitten.

For two years this deaf little cat with a fastidious distaste for both human and cat activity, refused to climb trees or submit to stroking but spent every evening curled up around Muffins's head, patting him on the nose with her paws or sleeping alongside him purring into his bulky warmth.

This companionship was one of the two attractive qualities she possessed – although she showed no desire to extend it out of doors, preferring (to my fury, since she was fond of using my wardrobe and even the inside of my shoes to deposit her evil little messes) not to leave the house at all.

Her other pleasing characteristic stemmed from her indifference to everyone and everything but Muffin. It made her quite bold. Although the other cats spat and shoved when she tried to eat, she ignored them. More than that, she was capable of thrusting her small, spotlessly white body right under Tiger's nose and eating his food. Hesitant as I am about anthropomorphic interpretation, I'm convinced that this indomitability made such a deep, if gradual, impression on Tiger, that after two years of ungracious tolerance he took her into his tutelage. Until that moment she had never ventured further than the front lawn or played with anything more challenging than a daisy. But one day to my astonishment I saw him, the lone hunter, plainly leading her down the back lane to his favourite observation point, an untrimmed bulge of hawthorn hedge just above the ford where he will sit for hours awaiting small, interesting movements.

Tail high, head occasionally turned to make sure Blot hadn't collapsed into her customary round, white sleep, he guided her to this precious place. Together, they sat side by side, tails twitching.

Later that afternoon I was outside reading some novel I had to review when, I heard, in the hedge behind me, a different note to the killer's yowl of either Tiger or Aurora. A smaller note altogether, but sharp with the same satisfied excitement. Blot wriggled through the hedge carrying in her neat pink jaws, a baby pygmy shrew. She tossed it up. Dabbed at it. Pounced. And crunched. Her initiation was complete.

From that day onward she has bounded up trees, stood on her hind legs to draw butterflies out of the air, looked up at the cry of fledglings, her small jaw quivering, and allowed herself to be stroked. Recently, she has taken to sitting on my lap and purring. I cannot account for it, unless perhaps her deafness helped reduce the acuteness of her instincts and she needed, more than other cats, to be shown how to act. Tiger no longer leaves the room if Blot appears. She has acquired her colours.

A favourite pastime of Blot's is to leap out from behind the privet and surprise a hen. If I were a cat I, too, should enjoy the sport excessively. The hen, whose comfortable, wifely

71

contour and continually busy food-gathering is only one heartbeat away from hysteria, reminds me irresistibly of the contemporary wife performing her conventional rôle with ill-suppressed alarm. In a detached way – with the ruthless observation of a novelist almost – Blot likes to trigger that alarm. The squawking, the flapping, the complete loss of dignified self-control is a matter of deep interest to her. She is not seriously concerned to attack or hunt, but simply to stimulate this fascinating response. One rocket-like entry of the hen into the air is quite enough to satisfy her.

I like my hens. I like their matronly presence about the place. I like the way they stand, wings slightly lifted, cooling their armpits in hot weather. I like the triumphant way they proclaim an egg is laid, although it's a fat-headed celetion since it pinpoints the place nicely. But I suspect it has a compensating purpose, for I've noticed that as soon as the cockerel hears a hen announce her marvellous act, he runs, neck outstretched, at Olympic speed to find her and attempt to mount her. Perhaps she is more receptive to him then though, if so, the receptiveness is of a purely physiological nature. I have never seen a hen appear to enjoy being mounted and no wonder, for the cockerel will seize the back of her neck to steady himself, and a small flock of hens dominated by an unduly active cockerel will look as wretched a collection of battered wives as you'll ever see outside the human kingdom.

Our first hens were a dozen elderly Marans handed on by somebody moving from the district. Large, darkly speckled birds, Marans lay enormous eggs, as brown as a sweet chestnut and four times the size. They don't lay as frequently as other common hens, but when they do, they leave a collector's piece in the nesting box, a splendour of proportion and colour.

We knew these hens had several laying years behind them and because we were unprepared for the length and misery of the annual moult, we feared the worst when, in the autumn rains and gales, they clung unhappily to protective walls, the grandeur of their feathers gone and their nesting boxes empty for eight weeks on end.

A year before we would have carried on throwing handfuls of corn in the kind thought that their end would at least be a natural enough affair. But this was the autumn of 1973, the months of the Arab oil crisis. It may sound absurd that events in OPEC determined a more brutal attitude towards our few ageing hens, but it does illustrate in little form, the general change high-priced energy was to effect.

To be perfectly truthful, John and I had already envisaged these changes. We could see that there would eventually be an oil shortage and that its implications for a massively fuel-consuming economy would be wide ranging and severe. Although it was obvious that the effects would be most immediately dramatic on high-technology industry and those employed in it, even more fundamentally worrying (so we believed) were the effects on food production in this country. A man needs food even more desperately than he needs work.

It had been part of our blithe expectation that John, as a competent gardener and I, as a somewhat less competent stockwoman, could usefully spend the five years we imagined it would take before the situation became really grave, learning enough about small-scale husbandry to then help start urban farming co-operatives. Self-sufficiency was never our aim. For one thing, you sound remarkably foolish talking about self-sufficiency in the countryside where everyone has always grown a large part of their own produce and never thought of attaching a fancy label to it. Secondly, and this was one of the objections we had had to the commune, self-sufficiency sounds (and is) smugly exclusive. A community *can* however be remarkably self-supporting in a far wider sense – in its borrowing and lending, its exchange of produce, clothes, and kindnesses, in its entertainments and its money-raising efforts for something the community is agreed it wants or needs. But this required no theory from us. It was alive and well in the place we came to and we, more than once, were humbled by it.

The five year plan we'd so confidently allowed for was

73

suddenly pulled from under us by the Arabs' artificial creation of shortage. We were caught short. We were in no way ready to offer helpful advice to others since we were stumbling around in the dark ourselves. It became increasingly clear that to finance our own modest researches, both of us had to keep working at whatever paid jobs were available. The possibility of John giving up his London job for something closer to home, where he could be of greater help to me, receded sharply. In any event, there was no other suitable work available. The price of animal feed shot up terrifyingly putting a number of small local farmers out of business over the following winter and making for us a harsher division between pets and functional animals. The first victims of the new, more stringent atmosphere were the unhappy Maran hens. If they had ceased to pay their way in eggs, then we had to face up to the economies of food production and eat the wretched things.

The decision was waveringly delayed. Then I saw an advertisement in the *Western Gazette*. Man would collect hens. Any number. Any time. Reasonable prices. We dithered while the hens continued to moan in the crevices of the cliff wall. Finally we reached a compromise. We would kill one and eat it to prove it could be done. The hen collector could take the rest.

One hen was selected as our Sunday lunch. The children were not to be told.

On the Saturday John plodded outside in the beating rain and grabbed our hen. So determined was he to do the job properly that when he pulled its neck the whole head came of in one hand, while its body flapped accusingly in the other. It was hung up and plucked.

"It might be rather tough," warned John gloomily.

On Sunday morning I began to casserole the hen: very early, very slowly. Its meaty fragrance stimulated no juices whatever, only a dry, funeral moss on the tongue. The hen collector failed to turn up at the promised hour so we released all the hens we'd kept shut in throughout the morning and watched them peck in a dilatory fashion at the grubs in the manure heap. Then, as the dreadful meal was about to be served, the hen collector arrived and John had to go and pursue every shrieking bird through the mud dropping them one by one, as he retrieved them, into the collector's paper sack.

We sat down to eat. The bird was quite unlike any other chicken I'd ever bought in its colour, taste and texture. It was brown and lean and chewy, somewhat stronger in flavour than the pale, bland bird of the supermarket deep freeze.

We picked at our plates.

"Is this one of ours?" Daniel examined a leg with curiosity.

John and I looked at one another. Truth was all. "Yes," I said tenderly, "I'm afraid it is."

"Not bad." Calmly Daniel continued working his way round the bone.

Later, while the children went outside to play war with their friends in the rain, we washed up in stricken silence. In the evening, the rain cleared and a thin sunshine bled out of the cloud. I went to clean out the hen house in preparation for a new flock. In one of the nesting boxes I discovered two large, glowing brown eggs.

Our next batch of pullets were plain brown creatures scientifically bred to lay. As so often when breeding is directed along very specific lines, a small, unforeseen flaw had erupted among the genes. Three of them promptly ran off down the back lane, jumped into the stream and were discovered there, legs upward, by Eddie Taylor's son, who kindly returned the corpses to us.

Once the remainder had started to lay though, they laid like machines and their outlines assumed that attractive and portly curve that comes from an enlarged egg-laying undercarriage. They clucked and scratched purposefully about the place and found all the same sheltered bowls of earth for their dust baths that the Marans had enjoyed before them, working away at a hollow beneath the cliff face among the ferns and hypericum and fluffing themselves out in the noonday warmth.

Occasionally, one would go broody and remain in her nesting box, feathers spread, burbling in a crooning fashion whenever you approached. When two went broody at the same time we bought them a goose egg apiece to sit on since we had no fertile hen's eggs of our own and we'd been told that geese raised by a mother hen developed a more equable temperament.

The principal mistake was moving them. A broody hen picks her place with deliberate and careful intention. If you want to discourage a hen from being broody and wasting three weeks singing sulkily to herself, I now know that the best thing to do is to move her. Cross and flustered, she'll complain for a while then, within a week, start laying again.

This however, was a logistical problem. A goose egg is a large thing. There is no room for both goose egg and hen in a nesting box so we removed both hens and egg into the stable. The hens were less foolish than I thought. They concluded fairly swiftly that if the egg they sat on prevented their feet from touching the floor, it was very probably none of their making. They climbed off and glared at the eggs from a distant corner of the stable.

"You want a damp sod," advised Hugh and dug up two squares of turf. "Put the eggs on there and shut the hens up in a confined space with them."

We wired off the front of a small metal coop and left the huffy mothers to their task. By morning both of them had energetically squashed the eggs and stood with an air of satisfaction, waiting to be released beside a mess of shell and yolk.

Since they were an excellent laying strain and I was beginning to sell a few surplus eggs, I decided to find a Maran cockerel who would give a little extra glamour both to the crossed offspring and the appearance of the eggs. Harlequin was my birthday present from John that year. A light and finely speckled young bird, he grew magnificently into a large creature with a comb as flamboyant as a national flag. He could be heard crowing for miles well before dawn.

To begin with, as he streaked at terriffic speeds, wings spread out, for the nearest hapless hen, he made me laugh. I was less amused by his attacks on the dog. When Harlequin rose in the air screaming, ruff extended, claws upraised to expose the curving spur, Muffin slunk away humiliated.

Next, the cockerel turned on me, pinning me against a wall as he flew at me, beak open, talons shaving my shins. I emptied buckets of water over him, kicked at him, even cracked the lungeing whip at him. He was violently undeterred. I became afraid to leave the house except on tiptoe and even then he would often smell my leaking terror from over a hundred yards away and hurtle towards the back door as I slithered inside, slamming it and watching him rise in a beating, squalling fury at my image on the far side of the glass.

"We've got to eat him," I said, sentiment totally scoured out of me by now.

"Look," rebuked John, "all you've got to do is approach him confidently. Show him who's boss. If he attacks, chase him. Easy. He never attacks me."

He showed me. As we shut the hens in that night, he shuffled Harlequin in front of him with his boots. "See?" he smiled turning towards me, palms outspread in confident demonstration. "Simple."

As he spoke, Harlequin sprang at John's back and ripped open his only decent suit.

I used to wait until it was after six o'clock and dark when the hens' own inner clock had turned them homeward to roost. Then I would creep up to the door of the shed, hurl the food in, slam the door and retreat.

He heard me coming. Waited for me. As the corn sprayed in he flew out shrieking. I banged the door of the hen house and fled from the run, managing to close the mesh gate before he grabbed me.

That evening we were visiting friends when I suddenly remembered that the cockerel was still outside the hen house. We hurried home through the darkness to find him. Even the

77

fiercest of cockerels is quiet enough to pick up while it's roosting, a characteristic others know well. Something had been there before us. All that remained of Harlequin was a scatter of feathers shining palely in the beam of our torchlight.

9

"**Y**OU *must* TAKE HIM CUBBING," LIZ INSISTED.

I'd had Solomon now for over a year. He had filled out, deepened and built up the muscle in his hind-quarters. He looked well. He'd attended classes for young horses in a covered school where he had started to negotiate small coloured jumps very well, considering the lack of help he received from his rider. But outside, on his own, he still napped badly, shying and firmly deciding wherever we were that no place compared with home.

"The only thing," Liz went on, "that will guarantee a young horse going forward willingly is hunting. It's an essential part of the training." She saw my face and continued. "It gives them confidence and courage and it's the only way they ever learn the judgment to cope with tricky jumps."

"Maybe," I intervened, "but . . ."

"If you don't open them up to new experiences," Liz said, ignoring me, "they get bored. Like children. And once a young horse is bored he just gives trouble. That's why he's messing you about so much. He's fed up with riding round and round the same old roads all the time. And *anyway*," she concluded with exasperated emphasis, "*you'd* enjoy it."

"I don't know about that," I replied darkly.

I still hadn't faced up squarely to my feelings about hunting. Quite apart from dull, practical considerations like time and expense, I felt a residual distaste for something dimly bound up with offensive social and political attitudes. The question of cruelty loomed less largely with me, though it wasn't entirely absent. I knew enough about the nature of foxes to appreciate the need to control them and enough about the different means of control to realise hunting was not the most cruel. But principally I think, I then felt that I shared no part of the gentry's lifestyle and outlook and didn't wish to pretend that I did. It was not a thing I could tactfully explain to Hugh or to Liz, both of whom had hunted all their lives and took it as much for granted as any other seasonal aspect of farming life. For them it was no more political than hedging and ditching, no more socially divisive than meeting one's fellow farmers at market. As breeders and breakers of horses, the hunting field was their schooling ground, a place where the capacity and heart of a horse could truly be judged.

"You're coming," said Liz, and started making arrangements for me to leave Solomon at their farm overnight so that we could ride the five miles to the meet together the following morning. "We'd better leave here at six," she ended briskly.

There was one further emotion tangled with all my other feelings on this matter . . . Fright. I knew that cubbing, unlike hunting, rarely involved much galloping about or jumping since the object of it is solely to train young hounds in their first season and indeed, to give young horses their first, un-alarming sight of hounds in a quieter and more relaxed at-

80

mosphere than the hunting field proper. All the same, when I arrived at the Holgates' farm at five the next morning and saw Solomon alerted to an unusual routine, I talked very very gently to him as I groomed him. My gut seethed.

A grey dawn broke as we clattered along deserted roads towards the meet. A thin mist overlay the fields.

"Look out for mushrooms!" cried Liz, well ahead of me on her enormous seventeen-hand four-year-old. She looked tiny on him, legs barely halfway down his ribs. It was his first outing too and I was heartily thankful that she, not I, had the task of acquainting this massive animal with the novelty of hunting.

"When you get there," she called over her shoulder, "keep him moving. Don't let him stand around getting up-tight."

My intestines knotted themselves as we wound through the lanes.

Through the mist I saw them gathered round a field of kale, horses whinnying in greeting, hounds leaping like porpoises above the green leaves and vanishing again below.

Solomon's head went up. He began to quiver all over. Instinctively, though quite wrongly, my hands tightened on the reins.

"Keep him moving!" warned Liz.

Keeping him moving was no problem at all. But persuading him to move in a quiet and steady fashion was another matter. He danced sideways. He threw his head about and seized the bit. He snorted in mock terror at the sight of so many horses weaving in and out of the mist. Trying to keep some distance from them, I walked him up and down the lower length of the field nearest the gate.

Voices called to one another in friendly recognition after a long summer's absence. I couldn't see their faces. I was too occupied gripping tightly on to the plunging back of my horse as he lowered his head and performed a flying buck. As the huntsman summoned his hounds, a horn sounded mournfully on the early morning air. The plangent note was too much for Solomon who responded with a half rear.

81

"Push him on!" Faintly, I heard Liz.

Then the entire field, horsemen and hounds, wheeled away from the kale and poured down the slope towards us. A hound shot through Solomon's legs as I tried to hold him back and let others pass. He reared right up this time and my tense restraint on the reins drew him over backwards on top of me.

"Loose horse!"

The cry went up as I lay on the hard ground and watched my horse careering through the gate away from me.

"I think that's probably enough for first time." Liz leaned down and held Solomon as I clambered back on trying to nurse a painful shoulder. "I'll come home with you," she said.

"No, no. You go on," I urged through clenched teeth. The whole episode had lasted no more than seven or eight minutes.

"Of course not, I'll come with you," Liz smiled kindly. "It'll be much better next time."

There had to be a next time. I *dared* not give the appearance of rank cowardice. Nor was I prepared to let that little horse have the better of me.

As soon as they met again within reasonable hacking distance, I grimly saddled up and set off hoping that the ride there would be so long my animal would be exhausted by the time we arrived.

If Solomon felt the least bit tired the sight of hounds revived him wonderfully. Gloomily and not very convincingly I forced myself to relax, keeping a good, clear space between myself and the rest of the riders. I saw the huntsmen, scarlet-coated, moving through the woodland trees, heard the curiously elegaic horn wind out of the covert and just let my horse gallop when the others galloped. After having remained in the saddle for a full twenty minutes without mishap, I retired.

Once more. Just once, to prove to myself that I wasn't merely inventing false excuses to cloak fear. My bowel liquidised, but I went determined to stay out for a full hour.

He behaved fairly sensibly. Able at last to give my attention to something other than staying on board, I ventured, with one eye, to see what cubbing was really all about. Not that I saw a single cub although I realised that the riders, ringed intently outside the covert, beating their saddle flaps with a dull, rhythmical thud of the whip were discouraging a hunted cub from breaking covert at the point where they stood.

The huntsman's grey horse crackled intermittently between the birches and a high, excited babble rose from hounds as a young deer sprang out from between the trees, free to go its own way. It bounded out of sight across the fields, its scut a white pennant in the mist.

A little of the sport's excitement had strayed into me. Something of its beauty. Obstinately, I tried to shut out whatever primitive exultancy dared trespass on my decent disapproval but when I rode home and a woman with a purplish, powdered face stopped her car to wind down the window and call out enquiringly, "Good morning?" I shouted "Yes!" with involuntary jubilance. Not, I supposed later, that it had, by normal hunting standards, been anything but the dullest of mornings, but I had passed an hour and a half in almost complete control of my horse. I had done what I felt was necessary. And (quelling the equivocal nature of my satisfaction) I need never go again.

Clearly there was little scope for extending the relationship between Solomon and myself. If his abilities were to be developed, I acknowledged that he needed to be hunted by somebody untroubled by scruples. I was not prepared to hunt for whatever inadequately confronted reasons and I was helped in avoiding the issue by wild rises in the commodity market that made feeding two horses properly more and more of a luxury. My cherished, lifelong fantasy had turned out to be a powerfully-willed little horse with more spirit than I had the skill to direct. He was, regretfully, for sale to the right person.

The right person appeared in no time. A girl who rode him with easy grace, who took him out for a full day's hunting and put him at a five-barred gate – an obstacle of a size and kind he'd never faced before – which he jumped like a stag.

Some months later I saw a photograph of him. It showed him gleaming and strong and I knew I'd made the right decision. But it hurt.

"Now you've only got that pregnant mare," observed Liz reproachfully. "I always thought you were mad to put her in foal. She'd have made the perfect hunter for you." She sighed over my foolishness. "Now you'll have to wait till next season."

Her persistence made me smile ruefully. As the winter landscape muddied under weeks of ceaseless driving rain, scent was reported to be poor. I bought a box of quarto paper and settled down to write a book.

IO

THE RAIN FELL MERCILESSLY. FIELDS LOW IN THE BLACK-more Vale lay under water for weeks and the road to Yeovil was regularly flooded. Winter hay ran short as cattle were kept in throughout March and then April. Some desolately stood out on the higher land, bare patches beginning to appear on their hide. Sowing was impossible in the waterlogged earth.

Bathsheba too stood out during the day, back to the wind and rain, head drooping. She looked huge and old, her winter coat matted with mud, her belly sagging. When I fetched her in at night she came quietly enough – too quietly – she was so submissive it seemed as though the heart had gone out of her. Apart from Joss Edwin's cattle whose field she shared, she was alone but it wasn't simply loneliness or even the

85

weight of pregnancy that dulled her, though certainly that slowed her and made her shift from leg to leg as she stood in the stable.

A month before she was due, the hormone pellet was located with some difficulty and removed and thereafter I watched her udder carefully to note whether it showed signs of filling. 'Bagging up' occurs a few days before foaling generally and when a waxy drop appears on the teats, you can be fairly sure that the birth will take place within forty-eight hours.

Mares tend either to foal very easily or with such difficulty the risk to both mare and foal is very great indeed. As the days drew on and the expected foaling date was passed I became very apprehensive about the chance of complications and my capacity to deal with them. John, who had been abroad a good deal that winter, was due to leave for Egypt at any moment and I couldn't rely on him for help. Instead I re-read every chapter on foaling in my large and ancient collection of horse books and assembled an irrelevant selection of first-aid items.

When she was ten days overdue, I brought Bathsheba into the little paddock nearest the house so that I could sit in my office and look up from my work through the runnelled window panes trying to detect any difference in her behaviour.

One dark afternoon in late April, as I squelched through the yard with food for the hens, I heard Bathsheba whinny. Surprised by the deep and protracted note of her cry, I ran to her. She whinnied again. It was the first time she had ever called for me.

She stood by the gate, nostrils distended, her neck hot under the cold, wet surface of hair. Peering down at her udder I saw it was so full that every time she moved, the insides of her hind legs were sprayed with milk adding to the streaks of mud and sweat.

Her anxiety, her clear need for contact of some sort, moved me terribly. After I'd heaped up plentiful supplies of clean, sweet-smelling straw in the loose box, I brought her in and she came gladly. We had met one another at last.

The flight to Cairo was postponed again. John came home. "It's going to be tonight," I said.

I rang the Holgates. "Tonight. It's going to be tonight."

"Leave well alone," advised Hugh. 'Let her get on with it. Look in about three in the morning if you must, otherwise let nature take her course."

At about eight, I carried a hay net into her. She snickered softly, pleased to see me. Her eyes were very large and lustrous, her neck dark grey with sweat.

"It'll be all right, my love," I whispered, running a hand gently over her before creeping out and stepping into a large puddle that had collected outside the door.

I watched television until close down. And then, at midnight, about to go to bed, I slipped out into the rain instead, just to stand outside the stable door and listen. In the darkness, beyond the steady rush of the weather, I heard heaving sounds. A straining, followed by a grunt. I waited. There was a slithering noise in the straw. A brief silence. Then a rustling of movement as the mare plainly rose from the straw and a series of soft, wondering whinnies.

She was still making small delighted cries of surprise when I stole quietly in. For a moment, she raised her head towards me to give a deeper cry of pride, then busily resumed licking the small, wet object at her feet. The foal, darkly plastered with amniotic fluid, lifted its head for a moment, then sank back. It was attached to the placenta by its cord. Since Bathsheba showed no sign of distress at my being there, I called John and together we waited to see that the baby could rise to its feet and suckle. It is absolutely essential that the foal absorbs the colostrum of the first feed within two hours of birth so that the foetal dung is cleared from its body. If the bowel movement fails to take place the foal can rupture itself, straining. It can die, even.

Vigorously, Bathsheba licked, restoring warmth to the small body and mumbling cries of encouragement as she worked her way from head to tail. Eventually the foal splayed out its long front legs and tried to rise (the tiny hooves were so pale and transparent they seemed barely formed). Then the hind legs – ridiculous, awkward props. It staggered and fell. Again it tried. And then again, with astonishing persistence. The cord would not break and each new attempt to rise was hindered, dragged back by the weight of the afterbirth. As the desperate efforts continued, the foal was visibly tiring and weakening and the thick white cord began to wind itself around the slender legs, creating a further obstacle. Still I waited, reluctant to go right into the box and touch the foal before it had fed in case my smell on its drying coat provoked Bathsheba to reject her baby. She stood, anxiously pushing at the infant with her muzzle, looking at us from time to time as if at a loss.

For two hours we waited. The intervals between the foal's attempts to stand grew longer. It lay flat out on the blood-stained straw, its small flanks heaving.

"We'll have to cut the cord," I said nervously having read what had to be done in such an emergency.

The scissors were sterilised, the iodine fetched. Cotton wool. Thread to tie round the cord. Bathsheba made no objection when we entered and knelt beside the foal. Firmly, John tied the ligature two inches below the navel and then made the cut. I applied iodine and dragged away the hampering mass of the afterbirth.

"It's a colt," I said.

Again we withdrew to the far side of the stable door and sat among the hay bales watching, full of silent worry.

The colt rose unsteadily, balanced and tottered instinctively towards the udder lips, sucking at the air, at his mother's elbow, at her belly, searching blindly for the right attachment. Suddenly, as he approached the udder, Bathsheba gave a cry of alarm and ran backwards away from him. He fell back weakly into the straw.

This desperate progress continued. Every time the colt neared her rear end she panicked, finally swinging away from him so violently, she knocked him to the ground.

Life was slipping out of the foal. He lay exhausted on the ground.

"She can smell us on him," I whispered distraught.

"Should we get the vet?"

"He *must* suckle," I muttered. "He *must* ..."

Bathsheba looked at us with consternation. She still licked her baby, still urged him to his feet. But again, as he tried one last time to stagger to the udder, she backed angrily away, ears flat. Her own confusion appeared to distress her and she looked pleadingly at us.

Any apprehension of the way she might react to me completely suppressed by the now urgent need to feed the colt, I resolved to milk her myself.

Letting myself into the box, talking quietly to her, I ran a hand gently over her quarters and bent to the teat. She stood rock still and let me milk off a little of the yellow colostrum into the palm of one hand. Then I slipped a thumb into the corner of the feeble little colt's mouth and poured the rich liquid down his throat. The operation was performed again and again, Bathsheba standing patiently as I relieved her full udder, then slipped its contents into the foal's mouth.

"Now, let's see."

We left them and stood on the far side of the door, watching.

As if by a miracle, the colt was reviving. So little of the thick, yellow milk had gone into him and yet he stood, more strongly now, the absurd, unbalancing length of his legs nearly mastered. Determinedly, he pressed towards the udder. Her head raised in alarm, Bathsheba swung away from him, grunting.

It was nearly five o'clock in the morning. Outside the rain beat down. Inside the stable Bathsheba's distress at her own failed instincts grew more marked. I continued milking. Every time I drew on the udder, she relaxed. With each new draught of milk the colt's strength and assertiveness increased.

Her willingness to let me touch her had puzzled me. Now I understood. I remembered her fear of gateways, her cautious hanging back whenever there were other horses close by. Now I suspected more strongly than ever that she had been so badly kicked or hurt by another horse at some time that her instinct to protect herself was over-riding her maternal instinct. But she, pathetically aware of some muddled conflict in herself, was full of anxious bewilderment.

Outside the square of window the clouds began to pale as morning came. I couldn't think what we were going to do. Totally weary, I was far too fearful of leaving her in case, in her consternation, she killed or injured the colt. For the moment, she depended on me utterly to fulfil her own distorted urge to feed him. He, in the meantime, his coat dried to a biscuity fluff, was purposefully committed to the idea of attaching himself to her.

Abruptly, as the sky lightened, Bathsheba herself worked out the solution. Backing herself hard into a corner of the box, quarters so tightly wedged into the wall that he couldn't possibly pass behind her, she waited for the colt to approach. He did. He seized the teat and sucked furiously. Gratefully, she let him.

Slowly, she relaxed and licked under his tuft of a tail while he fed. Her action seemed to prompt him, springingly, to raise his tail and the vital dung was passed.

It was all right. She settled peacefully in her corner. Her eyes half closed with bliss every time he renewed his hold on her.

We left them. It was nearly seven o'clock and still raining. I woke the children, told them the good news and cooked eggs and bacon for all of us.

I I

ALTHOUGH IT REMAINED BITTERLY COLD, THE RAIN LESS-
ened a couple of days after the foal's birth and the
moment the first watery sunshine appeared, I rushed
to bring Bathsheba and her colt outside. At two days old,
the colt was an odd stick insect full of charming curiosity.

We only dared as far as the lawn beneath the dripping
cliff wall that stretched alongside the stable. It was a nice,
safely enclosed space. In the few yards between stable and
lawn the foal encountered several startling pebbles and in-
sects from which he would have fled if his mother's comfortable rear hadn't continued to amble beyond these mon-
strosities. He tottered after her, reaching out his small muzzle
to examine interesting scents in the air.

Bahsheba, equally and powerfully divided between concern for him and lust for grass, tore at the lawn hungrily with a restless eye on her foal. Straddling his legs awkwardly in order to lower his head towards the juicy herbs, he sniffed at the grass. It was good. Joy made him spring upward and then he stopped, astonished by the agreeableness of his own action. Enraptured, he leapt again. Two paces, then three. His mother whinnied low and urgently as I held her loosely on the end of a rope.

The world was an excellent place. He sprang through the untidy grasses littered with plantain, buttercups and dandelions and galloped round her, falling flat on his side as he attempted a curve. Legs struggling in the air, he fought his way upright and set off again in the opposite direction, each new increase of speed ending in an unheeded tumble. Bathsheba swung round on her hocks, trying to keep him within the safety of her vision, eyes fixed anxiously on him as she bent her head for another snatched mouthful of grass.

After a short while John (still awaiting a flight to Cairo) led her back while I followed, my arms cradled round the colt's chest and quarters to guide him into the stable, where he instantly sank down into the fresh yellow straw and slept. Because of the clear delight he took in himself, because he was part of spring, because it is convention to try and merge the names of sire and dam, the colt was called Narcissus.

Bathsheba became a tender and contented mother who seemed, to judge from the lessening of her reserve towards us, to know that without us she might have failed. A closeness grew up between us. Although she remained wary of men in general, she rarely gave John any further trouble. To me she gave her total trust.

April and May are the weeks of birth. The air is thick with the overwrought cries and flight of birds. Walking up Charley Hill in the early morning or in late evening as the last of the sunlight unfurls down the slope and is caught sidelong in sharpened blades of grass, a succession of baby rabbits, uncertainly sensing a different presence, scurry one after the other into the brambles. White-faced Hereford-cross calves

92

caper beside their placid Friesian mothers, lambs suckle, the first blue-green tide of wheat appears, the cuckoo arrives.

I have seen a cuckoo at last, flying high above the trees at dusk, its long tail feathers narrowly speared and calling, still, as darkness falls.

The Holgates' goats produced only billy kids that year, quickly killed by Hugh who loathes this annual task for nothing rivals the charm of a kid, even the billy kid who swiftly grows into a stinking and generally foul-tempered animal. By seven months a billy can be sufficiently mature to father a kid of his own. As it often, but inexplicably, happens, everybody's goats seemed to be producing billies that year and I had difficulty finding a nanny kid for us. But Henry, who runs a small farm in the next village, had some goatlings – that is, year-old goats – to choose from. That's not quite accurate. Henry adores his goats and hates parting from them but his herd had expanded to such a size, his wife gently persuaded him that one fewer might not be a terrible loss. With some reluctance, he showed us two goatling sisters and recommended one of them. The other was afflicted with a spasmodic nervous twitch which might not augur well.

So we lifted Athene into the back of the Land Rover and took her home where, for the next three days, removed from her large family, she blared as only a goat can blare. It is a dreadful sound: the sound of a child having its arm slowly torn off except that mingled with the pain is a note of real grief.

It was so unendurable I asked Henry whether I might borrow the goatling with the twitch until I could find another kid to buy elsewhere as a companion for Athene. Lending, Henry seemed to feel, was all right. So Twitch came too and the blaring ceased. In the meantime, I heard of another kid that would be ready to wean in a month's time when Twitch could be gratefully restored to Henry.

Twitch and Athene are not pedigree goats. Basically they're British Saanens (with admixtures), white, shortish-haired goats descended from a Swiss mountain breed. Alpines, Toggenburgs and Anglo-Nubians are all more glamorous goats, some of them very beautifully marked and coloured, but their milk yield is markedly lower than that of the Saanen – a remark which will provoke raging argument amongst goat breeders, all of whom have the most violent reasons for preferring one type to another. As I said before, serious goat owners are an interesting breed in themselves. The local vets draw lots in their partnership, I think, to see whose unhappy duty it will be to take on the goat department. It's not simply that they admit to finding goats and their ailments a little mysterious, they find the owners wholly unfathomable.

There is something ancient and inscrutable about the goat. Its yellow eye with the black, oblong pupil gazes at you out of forgotten time. It possesses a single-minded, some would say wilful, streak which makes you sense that, like the cat, it has a clear memory of its own wild origin and that your proprietorship is something it is prepared to tolerate, to trade for a little extra food perhaps, but only on its own terms. Goats respond well, affectionately even, to those they judge worthy of them. Towards others they demonstrate a light-hearted disregard which is, I'm sure, the source of the furious dislike that so many who've had contact with them seem to feel for goats. For such people the goat's yellow stare is a terrible and baleful beam. It is the confident sneer of one's superior.

False beliefs grow as easily as briars round goats. Their shadowy presence in disreputable rites, on ancient Mesopotamian friezes, their sacrificial slaughter (the 'witch' of Wookey Hole, a nearby cave through which the green Axe pours, was principally identified thus, because her bones were found beside the bones of two goats – all three had starved to death) make them attract malicious rumour. Only the billy is ever vicious or smelly and billies are rare, although their smell is, I grant, so enveloping, so lingering, so musty and pungent that anybody sniffing it a hundred yards away from a herd of goats would justifiably imagine that the smell *must* be a collective one.

Again, contrary to belief, goats will *not* eat anything. They

94

will eat a good many things – vests, rose bushes, camellias, tea towels, young, but not old, dock leaves, nettles cut and withered for twenty-four hours, chocolate biscuits, pound notes, peas, beans, holly, the *New Statesman* and occasionally, grass. But they are not grazers. They are browsers and anyone buying a goat to keep their lawn neat will find their herbaceous border cleared, the bark of their trees stripped and their lawn luxuriantly long. Nothing pleases the goat's palate more than the bark and leaves of a young tree. John says goats are responsible for the wastes of the Sahara Desert. He says they are destructive and unmanageable. Sometimes, after they have made one of their frequent escapes into his vegetable garden, he says they should be shot. (The speed with which they can work down a row of raspberry canes is truly phenomenal.)

For one of the other characteristics of the goat – especially the mountain breed – is an ability to leap on to or out of almost anything. Visitors are often astonished to arrive and find goats jumping from the stable roof on to the top of their car or standing upright on a wall, heads buried among the sycamore leaves.

I find these qualities altogether engaging. John, who is an ardent vegetable gardener and grower of things, does not. The goats do not behave well for John. They refuse to budge when he tries to lead them, elude him when he flies full length after them in a rugger tackle, wait serenely as he builds a Colditz fence of barbed wire all round them, then lean on it until it is flattened.

The arrival of Twitch and Athene marked the beginnings of a bitter battle between John and myself. Finding it beyond us to enclose them reliably, we took to staking them on the end of long chains. Even these they seemed able, when determined, to drag out of the ground and more often than not they entangled one another so ingeniously in their chains that there was no peace until the bleating had been tracked down and the two goats (firmly yoked together) retrieved from a thorny hedge and freed.

In the running debate on goats that followed their arrival

I held firm. I conceded that cows do not wriggle under or over things with such ease, that they do not have to be brought in every night or rescued from a downpour, but, as I vigorously pointed out, they entirely lack the character of goats. John could find nothing whatever to delight him in the character of goats. Nothing *at all*, he repeated so often it became tedious. I hung on, certain that once they'd started producing milk he would be mollified. Goat's milk, he muttered, is filthy, thereby voicing another totally false belief.

There was some time to wait before my theory could be proved. A goatling shouldn't, ideally, be mated until she's sixteen to eighteen months old. Then there follows a very precise five-months' pregnancy. Although a maiden goat will often come into milk before she's kidded, it looked as though we'd have to survive a year of hostile wrangling before Athene was really able to recommend herself to John.

Meanwhile, my promised kid was weaned and at four months, came to us. Hollyhock, unlike the others, was horned which didn't, in her infancy, seem to matter very much and although Liz murmured ominously about the difficulties of keeping a horned goat the horns were very much to Hollyhock's advantage in the early months. Twitch to my great sorrow left (for in spite of her occasional nervous shuddering, she proved to have had a warmer, more interesting personality than her sister) and Athene, finding Hollyhock a dismal replacement, bullied the younger kid pitilessly. The horns gave Hollyhock the confidence she needed to withstand the constant battering. She was invincible. Athene finally resigned herself to her new companion.

It wasn't simply familiarity that inclined her to prefer Twitch. Goats have an unusually strong family feeling and they will accept a new goat that shares some of their own blood far more readily than a totally unrelated animal. Even after a lifetime spent together, unrelated goats will still maintain their differences and indulge in ritual butting or contests over food which they will share quite peaceably with sisters and cousins. This pronounced sense of family makes

96

them extraordinarily good aunts and substitute mothers to related kids. Few other animals would show the concern Athene was later to exhibit when her sister's babies were marooned and lost. Fretfully, she tried to work her way through the hole in the hedge where she knew they'd fallen. She even allowed one to suckle her. Their obstinate family loyalty appeals to me. It's very northern, somehow.

Hollyhock and Athene spent their summer skinning young willows, a maple tree, several old apple trees which recovered and one or two new ones which didn't. They pruned back the roses, finished off the magnolia we were trying to keep going in peat because the Somerset soil upset it, and harvested whole rows of runner beans.

"Why can't you get a cow!" complained John, close to tears as he surveyed his vegetable garden. "I can't take any more . . ."

The goats looked at him calmly, sharing a bough of hazel leaves, its plentiful crop of nuts still green. With great patience I rehearsed the drawbacks of a cow – chiefly that it would eat far more grass than we'd got and give far more milk than we needed.

"I hold you responsible for this!" shouted John, indicating the stalky remnants of his beans and brassicas.

"It'll be all right, you'll see," I promised. But then the Clarkes came to stay.

12

My God, you don't keep goats!" Robin Clarke glared
malevolently at the goats. They responded by crouching their quarters and urinating forcefully on the
ground.

Janine laughed. "They're dreadful," she said.

The Clarkes' commune in Wales had broken up after two
years. From the way they were talking I assumed the crisis
had arisen over goats. Later, it became clear that this had
been a minor quarrel compared to the one provoked by the
psycho-therapeutic fervour of the man with polystyrene pillars.

"You ought to get a cow," Janine advised. I thought her
disloyal but was so pleased to see her, I let it pass.

We spent an agreeable few days with only a limited number of references to the superior qualities of the cow.

"There's the cream . . ." (Cream, in goat's milk, is dispersed. It doesn't rise to the surface as it does in cow's milk, which makes it difficult to separate.)

"You can make butter . . ."

"I don't want to make butter. I can buy it far more reasonably than I can make it."

"You can just leave a cow in a field no matter what the weather."

"We don't have a field large enough to maintain a cow."

"It depends what sort of cow you buy."

"I'm not buying a cow."

We went to Shaftesbury market for a day out. I was looking for a Rhode Island cockerel but since there was no poultry at the market I left the others and went into the town to do shopping. On my return I found them grinning.

"We've bought a cow," John said.

"You've *what*!"

"So you can see the advantages for yourself. Only experience is going to convince you."

They went on grinning. I was absolutely furious.

"Right," I ground out with extreme lack of charm, "she's *your* responsibility. *I* keep the goats.'

They returned home later that afternoon with Jasmine in a trailer. She was an exceptionally pretty cow in rather poor condition. I burnished my indifference.

"In calf," said Robin triumphantly.

"So she's not actually going to *give* any milk until when?" I enquired scornfully.

Robin cast an expert eye over her. "Oh, I shouldn't think she'll calve till about November." It was then July.

"You'd better learn to milk," I said sweetly to my husband. I wasn't behaving very well, but then neither was he. "You'll have to come all the way back from London every morning and every evening to do it." Goats had brought us to this.

Jasmine mooed wretchedly and my heart puckered with guilt. It wasn't her fault.

"Anyway," I persisted grumpily, "what makes you think she's a house cow? She's probably been kept in a herd. She's probably never been hand milked in her life. Where does she come from?"

"The Isle of Wight."

"What's so wrong with a cow that she has to be sent to a market as far away as Shaftesbury?" I wanted to know.

"Oh, she'll be all right." Together, Robin and John began to her towards the paddock.

"We haven't enough grass for a mare, a foal, a cow . . ."

"Come on there!" They made farmerly sounds at the cow.

". . . And two goats."

As I've explained before, our back paddock borders on Joss Edwin's fifteen-acre field. Beyond the thicket of hazel and ash that grows out of the once layered hedge dividing us, a herd of Friesian heifers grazed peacefully. Jasmine made for the hedge at a purposeful trot, heaved herself through it and, showing a surprising turn of speed, galloped uphill towards the heifers. Robin and John watched in silent dismay.

They pursued the sprightly cow for some time.

At length, Joss Edwin arrived for the daily check on his cows. He gazed reflectively on the pursuit. Once caught, Jasmine would not lead but broke away again trailing her rope. Next time one of them made a succesful grab for her, she leaned her weight heftily against that of Robin and John. Janine and I were weak with laughter.

"You want to hold her tail up," said Joss and showed them how. By this means she was brought back into the paddock.

Sweating with effort, Robin and John repaired the gap in the hedge. No sooner was it mended than Jasmine discovered a fresh weak spot and made off again.

In all she made three bids for freedom before we finally shut her in the stable. Robin and John spent all the following day fencing the back paddock securely. They seemed to appreciate the funny side of the episode with a certain stiffness.

One gilded early morning when only the dovecote, raised on its own small hill, floated above the valley mist, I went out to feed the hens and discovered Jasmine asleep in the vegetable garden, sated.

After a while she settled. Because I had to feed her extra corn to improve her condition, she very swiftly came to my call. Most cows – especially herd animals which she had certainly been – are very timorous which is why I'm always appalled when I hear people express terror at the prospect of walking through a field of cows (even if there's a bull in the field, as long as he's running with his cows, he'll do no harm). Jasmine, however, was uncommonly friendly, eagerly coming to push her dark muzzle against me in hope of food and rasping her tongue across the palm of my hand. It was rather annoying in the circumstances. Her pale gold hide bloomed and, as she filled out, her pregnancy became more evident.

"I think she'll calve before November," I remarked, looking at the drooping curve of her belly.

John was busy preparing to spend two weeks living off the bare land of Exmoor for a film he was making on survival. The air was filled with the sound of his flint-napping. "Stone Age man must have had a lot of time to spare," he said gloomily, surveying the mis-shapen flakes of flint strewn all over the yard.

'I think she'll calve fairly soon," I repeated.

"I'm going to practise trapping rabbits instead," he said, rising stiffly to his feet.

"Suppose she calves while you're away?"

"September?" he said, "I doubt it. You know, I think we'll have to cheat and take a knife on this expedition."

Richard Mabey[1] came down to spend the preliminary weekend on Exmoor with John to search out the survival party's edible possibilities. He returned on the Sunday evening looking aghast. (John had remained behind to start his fortnight's filming.)

[1] Author of *Food for Free, The Unofficial Countryside.*

101

"There's nothing," said Richard, peeling off his soaked anorak, "not even a blackberry."

The two wettest weeks ever recorded in September began. The roof flew off the field shelter and flapped noisily in the back lane. A branch of the elm came crashing down and blocked the path between lower and back paddock. I sawed away at it and dragged at it piece by piece while the rain sheeted down inside my clothing. Every bit of corrugated iron round the place crashed like timbrels. Jasmine was curled up in one, unprotected corner of the remaining field shelter on that summer's wet, black hay.

I hauled the branch clear, put my saw down and went to look at her. As I drew near, I saw a small, dark form tucked into her flank. She had calved. Mooing lugubriously, she tried to use her body to shelter her black Angus-cross calf from the cruel downpour. Normally one wouldn't worry much about animals giving birth in bad weather but this was exceptional – the calf was growing cold and had to be brought indoors. Fortunately, she trusted me and allowing me to pick the small but weighty creature up, she followed me as I walked slowly backwards down the hill in a crouched position holding the calf as close to her muzzle as I could. Since there was no trace of afterbirth I imagined she'd eaten it already but I was glad to have her indoors anyway to make sure she cleansed properly.

So, I sat in the clean straw watching her lick her baby and laughed at the irony of it. There was John, totally inaccessible, scratching for food and shelter on bleak, exposed moorland and there was I, facing the udder of his cow. He couldn't have avoided the issue more plausibly.

A cow's udder is a more sizeable proposition than a goat's and it was some time since I'd practised. Sitting on an upturned bucket with my glasses on to make sure I could see what I was doing, I began.

Milk spurted down my trousers, in my ear, all over my glasses, through my hair. My wrists and fingers ached as I moved from one teat to another. As one emptied, another

102

filled up. My first attempt took an hour. At the end of it I was filthy, sticky and rancid smelling. Although the calf would gradually take more for itself, the idea of undergoing this performance twice a day was deeply depressing.

It is usual to take the calf off the mother in a matter of days to keep the maximum yield. The calf is then either hand-reared or marketed for slaughter. I hadn't a clue what to do and for the moment milked off two gallons a day and left the remainder for the calf. The first milk, called the beystens, I poured into a dish and baked. It set like a firm, rich custard. The cats thought it delicious. No one else could eat it.

Considering she'd never been hand-milked, Jasmine submitted very sweetly to my fumblings, only occasionally giving an impatient stamp or knocking over the bucket. She had a horrible but unintentional habit of defecating, then flicking her fouled tail back and forth across my face as I learnt to squirt more accurately. It took for ever and I had to have a bath after every session.

The bull calf, which somehow became named Hernia, was a compact little animal, already strongly grown when John returned gaunt and ill from his two dreadful weeks on Exmoor. Another day and I don't think he would have survived. I felt he'd done so bravely to stick it out in that Biblical weather I gave him time to recover before suggesting that he should now milk his cow.

Jasmine turned her glamorous golden head towards him as he settled down on the upturned bucket, gave him a sound flick with her filthy tail and promptly refused to let down any milk at all.

"She doesn't seem to want to . . ." John squeezed and a painful trickle emerged, then nothing. "I'm afraid you'll have to do it," he said humbly.

Foolishly we had left Hernia on his mother. He grew greedier and bolder, creeping easily underneath the post and rail fencing to explore his surrounding. Every time he wandered away Jasmine bellowed for him frantically until I chased him back. This happened so many times in the day that I

103

was getting very little work done and growing very exasperated. Moreover, as the calf required more and more milk Jasmine grew less and less willing to let me take any, becoming very restive as I milked her. There were fewer bottles topped with thick, custardy cream in the fridge.

Hernia's spirit of adventure increased as our milk ration diminished. He took to quite long journeys abroad, disappearing for two hours at a time, while his mother kept up a loud and rude lament.

"She's got to go," I decided. "Or the calf must, anyway."

Henry said he'd gladly relieve us of the calf.

The following day both Jasmine and Hernia vanished. Made desperate by her calf's exploring, Jasmine discovered that if she wriggled hard enough, she, too, could just squeeze under the post and rail fencing. She was reported in the town, last seen going round the one way system the wrong way.

I herded her back. An hour later, Mr. England, the builder, came up the drive.

"I've just seen your cow in the High Street," he said helpfully, adding as I hurtled downhill for the second time that day, "I bet when you were in London you thought it'd be lovely gazing out of the window at your quietly-grazing cows."

I couldn't even smile.

"They've both got to go," I said to John when he came home.

He drove her to market next day. I wept with guilt over our clumsy failure. Jasmine's yield was now so much reduced she was unlikely to be bought as a milking cow.

The only good thing to come out of the whole sorry event was that Henry agreed to swap Twitch for Hernia and so she returned to join her sister. I now had three goats, two of whom would soon be ready to be served by the billy. But instead of enjoying the triumph of an argument won, I sat and grieved over Jasmine. I'd dealt stupidly with that nice creature and feel shabby about her still.

104

13

AS THE SUMMER LENGTHENED NARCISSUS GREW INTO A
strong and lively colt, a local centre of attraction for
the stream of visitors, young and old, who liked to
hang over the fence and remark on his beauty. As his foal
fluff had worn away he emerged a gleaming bay, the same
honey-toned colour as his father.

Like any intensely proud mother, Bathsheba was ridicu-
lously tolerant of her son's behaviour, his greedy sucking, his
nibbling of her tail and the barging use he made of her to
slow his headlong gallops, but by late September, as the
leaves began to crackle underfoot and the grass was reduced
to bare patches, the dreaded moment of weaning was drawing near. Mother and foal, oblivious of it, moved slowly
across the field, heads down, trying to eat the same blade

of grass. I watched them guiltily knowing what was in store and fearing that by separating the two I would forfeit the trust Bathsheba had at last invested in me.

Of all the tasks to do with animals, weaning is the one I like least of all. The distress of the mother, the bewilderment of the infant tear me to shreds. It is also a wickedly complicated business, or was for us, at least.

In a sense the preparation had started very early, when Narcissus was a week old and had been taught, with Jack Hopkins' help, to lead independently. A foal slip – a soft, webbing headcollar – had been carefully fastened round his head with much crooning and scratching of ears and then two leads, one on the near side, a longer one on the off side which ran round the length of his body and behind his quarters, were attached. Once he was accustomed to the sensation I walked ahead with Bathsheba while Jack followed on behind cradling the colt and murmuring "Good little lad, good little boy, good little lad . . ." as sweetly as if he'd been soothing his own baby. Jack likes to present himself as a tough man and talks a lot about the need to handle animals firmly, but, as we wove an unsteady line through long grass alight with ox-eye daisies, that big tall man was the essence of gentleness.

Over succeeding weeks, the education advanced slowly. Cissy would be shut in the stable while I led Bathsheba a few yards away, a little further each day, before returning her to Cissy, who was wheeling round and round the stable or trying to clamber over the door.

Now, as the sycamore leaves fell in the yard, the arrangements for parting had to be made more absolute. First of all, it was necessary to find a field far enough away from home for mare and foal to be out of earshot of one another. Secondly, each had to be found a new companion to help them settle until it was again possible to put them back together – six months would probably be long enough for the bond to be sufficiently broken and Narcissus rid of the desire to suckle his mother.

All was effected. Bathsheba was to be taken over Charley Hill to Brick Kiln field where Emily, another grey mare be-

longing to a friend, would help distract her. To lessen the
shock as much as possible, Cissy, after two days spent shut
up in the stable, was to be kept in the paddock at home with
a pony called Clopper. Once the two pairs had accepted
their new circumstances, they would be swapped over so that
Bathsheba could be brought back home and ridden again
in order to get her fit. "To get her fit for hunting," Liz had
remarked. Fit, anyway. She was as soft and fat as a feather
pillow.

It proved every bit as horrible as I'd feared it would.

John led Bathsheba away over the hill – partly because I
couldn't face the treachery of it and partly because he was
strong enough to cope with her if she fought to be restored to
her baby. They reached the field without trouble but once
there, she charged up and down screaming with anguish,
pausing only to stand briefly by the gate and strain for an
answering call before she plunged away on a further crazed
circuit. The other mare, separated from her temporarily by
a gate, offered no comfort at all and after satisfying her
curiosity with a look in Bathsheba's direction, grazed im-
perturbably.

Cissy, too, kept up a ceaseless cry behind closed doors and
when I eventually put him out with the pony, the nasty little
beast went for him squealing and lashing out with real purpose. The attack went on all night. In the morning when,
sleepless, I went out to see what state of relationship they'd
reached, Cissy hung back terrified. Every time he tried to
come to me for comfort, Clopper chased him off.

"Give them time," John said. "They'll be all right."

The screaming and squealing lasted for another three days.
In the meantime Bathsheba refused to make accommodation
with Emily whom she clearly suspected of stealing her baby.
She stood alone by the gate, her eyes huge with agitation.
It seemed better that I should start working her straight
away to take her mind off her loss. The complicated swap-
over was put into operation. Bathsheba was caught and,
after several powerful attempts to break away, was saddled

and ridden the long way home along the road while, above us, John and Daniel led Cissy and Clopper over the hill to Brick Kiln where they were awaited by an evil-looking Emily not at all pleased to share her grass with two others.

That was done on the Saturday – in those days everything major had to wait for a weekend when John was home – our weekends became laden with crisis. On the Sunday morning after bringing Clopper back to occupy Bathsheba, I went to church, and walked home later in pouring rain to find Emily's owner waiting for me at the bottom of Providence Place, her face wild and swollen with tears. "There's been an accident!" she blurted out. "Cissy . . ." she started.

I ran past her, suddenly sick.

A grave-faced knot of people hung about in the yard, their wet clothes clinging to them. Inside the loose box, Jack Hopkins held Cissy, talking to him softly and rubbing his neck. Both of the colt's hind legs were ripped open to the bone. He was bleeding badly.

"There little lad, steady now, easy now . . . steady . . ." Jack was murmuring. He saw me. "I've rung for the vet," he said.

While we waited and I stared aghast at the damage that had been done, Jack explained what had happened. Not, I suppose, realising that the pony had been removed from Brick Kiln, Emily's owner had taken her mare out of the field for a ride and Narcissus, finding himself alone, had panicked, attempted to follow and tried to jump a big metal gate. Unable to clear it, he'd crashed right through it, breaking the gate and tearing his legs back to the tendon. The bone gleamed through, pale blue.

Jack, who had been out exercising his dogs nearby, was able to run to the rescue before Cissy floundered into the main road after Emily and, finding that the colt was able, very stiffly, to walk, had led him back home over the hill, whereupon Bathsheba, seeing her foal, had begun an unbroken trumpeting call that went on still. Every time she thundered the length of the paddock above us, Narcissus, head tensely raised, whinnied back to her.

The injuries looked so serious I dared not think what the outcome would be. I stroked the little colt's neck and felt his muscles rigid as iron.

The vet took one look and rang for another colleague to come and help him. While we waited I tried to guess from his face whether he thought there was hope, but I couldn't ask. He, too, was very silent.

The two vets conferred and decided to try and cobble together what shreds of skin were left. Cissy was given a full anaesthetic and within seconds, keeled over into the straw we'd piled up beneath him. I knelt, holding his head, watching for any conscious fluttering of the eyelid.

As the two men crouching over him worked swiftly and silently, cutting, cleaning, stapling with metal clips, Bathsheba's hooves drummed sonorously overhead, her calls seeming fainter – perhaps because our own concentration was tightly drawn to the centre of what we were doing, perhaps because the rain fell ever more heavily on the roof above.

It took a long time.

Had any of the tendons been severed there would have been no choice at all but to destroy him. As it was, there was just a chance – because he was a young and healthy animal – that the wounds might heal by first intention.

Over the next ten days, until the stitches could be removed, the vet came every morning to dress Cissy's legs. On the tenth day, when the stitches were taken out, it was clear the wounds had not healed as was hoped. The flesh had turned proud and was suppurating.

"It's going to be a long job." The vet looked up, disappointed. He'd tried his absolute best. The colt's legs would need re-dressing and bandaging twice daily for some time to come, too difficult a job for me to manage on my own. It wouldn't be easy for one person to deal with an older experienced horse in such pain, but with a baby like this, unused to having a leg picked up for any length of time and being asked to support his weight on three legs, one of which hurt dreadfully, a baby still suffering all the shock of being weaned, it required up to three people to soothe, hold and

109

attend to him. At the vet's suggestion, Cissy was moved to his surgery in the next village which involved yet another new and frightening experience for him: being put in a trailer and bounced down the steep rutted hill while trying to keep his balance on injured legs. But he survived it. He was away for a month and in that time, the bright, bold little colt who'd bounded so confidently round his mother all summer long, turned into a dull-coated, despondent animal, his hocks raw where he'd tried to bite away the bandages, his neck a weak, inverted U-shape. He looked like a little mule.

To sustain so many shocks in so short a space of time was a real test of his temperament. And although he looked awful, throughout the entire time he spent closed up in a stable barely able to move, standing on painful legs, enduring the discomfort of daily treatment, he never lost his sweetness of spirit nor showed any resentment of the human beings whose presence must have been associated in his mind with pain.

By November he was able to come home. For the next three months he patiently allowed me to bathe and bandage his raw, blemished legs every day, sometimes without even being tied up.

"Few youngsters have had that much handling," reflected Jack, who came often to see him. "He'll be no trouble to break when the time comes."

There were incidental problems, minor in relation to everything else that had been overcome, but things to be considered nonetheless. One was that he had to be stabled next door to his mother (now clipped out for the winter months and gradually losing her slack outline as daily exercise sharpened her up). Although, technically, Narcissus was weaned, this nearness meant that the psychological bond between the two animals was still very strong and on Bathsheba's part, urgently tender. The other fact to be faced was that any scheme I'd entertained of selling my colt to recoup some of the (now alarmingly large) expenditure was out of the question. Nobody would dream of buying a young damaged horse. Although I frankly had no desire whatever

110

to part with him, if he *were* to be saleable it meant keeping him until he was at least three, probably four, when he could be broken, schooled and prove something of his worth. In the two years I had now kept horses, the price of hay and straw had doubled and the price of feed trebled. All it meant was that I had to spend considerably more time at my typewriter and dashing back and forth to London doing various television programmes than I'd bargained for. I was fortunate, of course, that I could earn the extra money and, somehow my family organised itself in such a way that nobody suffered extreme neglect. The problem of keeping Bathsheba exercised and fit was solved for me in the ambiguous way of fate, by her going helplessly lame.

I'd been aware of her reluctance to leave home when we went out in the early mornings but thought it was unwillingness to leave Cissy behind. Slowly, though, as her condition worsened, it became clear something more physical was troubling her. Whatever it was, it was extremely hard to define. I suspected something in the right fore, the vet suspected something in the left and froze the lower leg off with anaesthetic to see if she then went sound. She didn't, so attention was transferred to her shoulders. Probably, the vet thought, a muscular strain of some kind.

"She'll need six weeks' rest," he advised, adding sympathetically that I didn't have a lot of luck with my horses.

So, after two months of gradual exercise, first walking then building up to a steady trot, she now had to be 'let down' again, her feed reduced, her winter coat allowed once more to grow.

"Oh no," groaned Liz, calculating how long it would take to rest Bathsheba, then bring her back into a fit state again. "Three months. The hunting season will be over by then."

I have to confess to a minor seepage of relief at that. A couple of weeks later, Liz rang. "I've got an idea," she exclaimed enthusiastically. "Taffy the Back. He'll fix her."

Taffy turned up one wet, black winter's night in January.

111

"It's a bit dark," I observed doubtfully. "You won't be able to see the mare move."

"Oh, don't want to see her *move*," he said in a strong Welsh accent. "It'll only confuse me to see her *move*."

Slightly puzzled, I blundered ahead of him through puddles, a raincoat over my head. Taffy, a small figure, lumbered after me carrying a large and heavy box. At least there was light in the stable now. I didn't mention Bathsheba's unpredictable response to strange men.

"I think it's her shoulders," I said helpfully.

Grunting, he put his box down, walked straight up to the mare, blew vigorously up her nostrils and ran his finger tips all over the shoulder area. "Right," he said, as if the offending part had been located.

He bent, lifted up the mare's left foreleg, pulled it out straight, then doubled it up at the knee against his chest and rocketed her backwards across the stable with the force of his own slight weight. He then did the same with the right leg. Bathsheba catapulted into the corner a second time without a tremor of protest.

Next, the large black box was unpacked. It contained an impressive array of ultra-violet electrical equipment, a superior version to the thing my grandfather had used to stimulate hair growth on his very bald head. I could remember the purple flashes of light and the crackling it gave off while the massage was performed. Taffy's massage machine, so he said, transmitted a very high speed electrical charge. The mare drowsed while he ran it over her shoulders for an hour. We talked.

Taffy had been a jockey. It was either that or the mines. Size had determined his choice of career. Born in a mining valley during the Depression, the youngest of twelve children, he hadn't grown properly. "There wasn't a lot of food," he said.

He'd won a reputation as the jockey who'd ride anything, which is why he'd had more falls than most, riding bad horses. Every bone in his body broken twice over, he'd finally broken his back and lain paralysed for six months in Stoke

112

Mandeville. After that, he'd healed horses. He had the gift. His father, a miner, had possessed the gift before him. He'd been the local bone-setter. "Every Sunday, people came from miles around to have him put them right again."

Taffy mostly worked with racehorses, treating strained tendons with vinegar and brown paper and dancing on their slipped discs.

"Give me a leg up would you?" he asked when his machine had finished its humming.

He was as light as a feather. He sat and then sprang upright on Bathsheba's back, feeling along the length of her spine with his feet. When his toes detected the doubtful vertebra, he leaped in the air and landed quite forcefully. Apart from a surprised, sagging grunt, Bathsheba stood like a rock.

It was quite a display. He slid down, patted her, blew again up her nostrils and said, "You must ride her now. Make her move. Make her use herself. She's got a psychological block about using herself, see, she's known pain so she expects it. I want you to take her up and down hills, ride her in circles, starting large and growing smaller until she can see she has nothing to worry over." He patted her reassuringly. "In three days," he said, "she'll be sound again, you'll see. Will you ring me and tell me?"

I promised I would.

We'd talked about Narcissus and he was interested to look at him so I unbandaged the colt's legs and Taffy gazed at the raw, misshapen limbs. Standing so long indoors trying to spread his weight more comfortably, Cissy had become 'cow-hocked', pinched in at the hocks and splayed out at the feet.

"You want to leave those bandages off now," said Taffy. "Smear his legs with honey and turn him out in the field during the day."

He stayed, talking long into the evening and asked apologetically for five pounds before driving the forty miles back to his home in Gloucestershire.

Dubious as I was, I did everything he asked. Bathsheba groaned audibly at every step she was asked to take downhill. Even more dutifully, I smeared Cissy's legs with honey and

113

turned the pair of them out together. Cissy stood by the gate disbelievingly for a moment. Cautiously, he took three paces forward. Then, head raised to absorb the chilly freshness of the air, his whole body shook as he gathered himself for the first wonderful leap. Freedom went to his head. He couldn't bear to stop his weird and marvellous gallop, hind legs moving in unison like a rabbit's, each, I suppose, unable to sustain too much weight individually. He and Bathsheba raced, manes flying, wheeled and raced again until exhausted, he slowed and stood, head high, tail raised like a plume, and blew long, exultant snorts before dropping greedily upon the poor but precious winter grass.

For the next three days he was so stiff in the morning that he had to be heaved to his feet and there he stood looking hopefully over the stable door in anticipation of another unfettered day in the outside world.

On the third day, Bathsheba was sound.

"Good," said Taffy over the phone, not at all astonished. "Given her back her confidence, see."

When, several months later, Taffy heard through Liz that Bathsheba had gone lame yet again, he called one evening while I was away working in London and it was John's turn to witness the extraordinary, tangible bond the Welshman instantly established with that wary old mare.

"He refused to take any money," John told me later, marvelling over Taffy's dancing. "Absolutely refused. He said he just wanted to see she was right."

14

ACCIDENTS ALLEGEDLY HAPPEN IN THREES AND THEY DO have a weird way of living up to their triple reputation. Shortly after Narcissus injured himself and had to be brought back to the foaling box, he was joined by two other ailing creatures.

One was a Silkie bantam cockerel who seemed to have been reduced to a neurotic, grieving torpor by the death of his 'wife', she having drowned herself in the water trough. He withdrew into a corner of the foaling box and closed his wings around himself in evident misery. One of three bantams I'd been given (all of them small, exquisite birds with feathered legs), the cockerel was bridegroom white save for his luminous blue dewlaps and a crushed raspberry formation attached to the top of his beak. Unlike the drowned wife, who had also been pure white, the third bantam (a Silkie cross) was a soft golden colour, darkened at the wings by black, lacy markings. The children called her Solo because her independence, an improbable quality in a hen, was so marked. The cockerel took no further interest in her and shortly after his bereavement, in a moment either of carelessness or abandoned hope, also drowned himself and was discovered floating in Cissy's bucket like some sad, trailing water plant.

Solo promptly turned gloriously broody and sat on the clutch of small, blueish bantam eggs until three pure white chicks were hatched. A faultless and delightful mother, she reared two cockerels, far less hysterical than their father had been and a little white hen who was, with her, to become constant nurse and mother to chicks hatched from eggs laid by our larger brown hens. Solo's refusal to move from her clutch of fertile eggs over a period of nearly four weeks and her later defence of her chicks from the hostile curiosity of both the larger hens and our cats, was a fierce and devoted example of parenthood. I have seen her double the size of her small neat body by raising every feather from its root and then fly at a horse who dared push its muzzle in the direction of her brood. Once she ran squawking to find me when yet another chick tipped over the edge of a bucket and had to be rescued and dried in front of the fire. The other hens, who normally push the bantams to the further edge of their pecking circle, made way for Solo as though the largeness of her personality impressed them as much as it impressed me.

The other convalescent in the stable was Athene who, the day after Cissy's accident, fell down and turned blind. A course of Vitamin B injections helped her recover a little of her co-ordination but her senses of smell and sight were feeble for some time and she staggered pitifully round the stable searching for her food. It was quite impossible to keep her with the other goats who jostled indifferently past her but Cissy was content to share his feed bucket with her. At other times he stood patiently as she supported herself against his front legs. It was a reciprocal arrangement they had, for when the time came for him to go to the vets and be led into a trailer it was she who encouraged him by going up the ramp first and swaying with him the length of a journey that must have been deeply alarming, as branches dragged across the roof and rasped the sides of the trailer on its uneven descent downhill.

My goats enjoy travelling. I'd discovered this unexpected pleasure in Athene a few weeks before she fell ill and we'd made our first journey in search of a billy.

From August onwards I'd kept a sharp eye on the two nannies, now old enough to be mated, for some sign of their coming into season. Since a goat can come into season for as brief an interval as half an hour, you have to be prepared to act fast. It was easy, so Henry had told me, to observe the signs. The goat keeps up a persistent blaring. Her genital area swells and her tail flickers as if a bee has lodged itself beneath it.

At last Athene twitched her tail, inflamed by a delicious irritation. Within twenty-four hours I'd located a billy in Glastonbury. For reasons too tedious to explain, the excursion involved loading Athene, four children, two adults and myself into the Land Rover late in that autumn afternoon. The children were dropped off at the bottom of Glastonbury Tor as they said they preferred to spend the next hour playing there, while John, I and eighty-three-year-old Alice Bunn continued on our way with Athene. Alice Bunn is very game but once levered into the Land Rover found it simpler to stay there and seemed thoroughly to enjoy this unusual expedition.

We discovered the billy's owner in a council house commune and he led us to a wild patch of land where he kept a dozen or so very mixed goats. In light that was failing fast, he caught his best billy and we retired with our respective animals to a wired-off enclosure where we let them acquaint themselves with one another.

That was my first smell of billy. I now know that measured on a scale of ten, that particularly billy would register a mere two, but at the time I thought it chokingly rank.

117

After a little foreplay Athene faced the Glastonbury Billy, fixed him with a basilisk stare, lowered her head and butted him so hard he sat abruptly on his haunches, eyeballs swivelling like beads on an abacus. Darkness was falling.

"I'm terribly sorry," I said to the dimming figure of the billy owner. "She doesn't seem to be in season any longer. Perhaps I could call back in three weeks or so?"

"Certainly," responded the young man, comforting his dazed animal. "Any time." He gave a weak smile and waved us goodbye.

Athene stood in the back of the Land Rover nibbling Alice Bunn's hat while we drove off to find the children. They were not, as I'd asked them to be, waiting at the foot of the Tor. It was now night and a full moon shone round and white behind the tower of St. Michael's Church, high on the peak of the Tor.

"Hang on," I said handing Athene to John, and began the steep climb up, crawling every now and then on my hands and knees. Far above me, close to the moon, I could hear the faint clamour of children.

So much time had passed by the time I reached the top, gathered the children and started the downward slide that halfway down we met John, anxiously coming to find us. Athene trotted beside him on the end of a rope. "I couldn't leave her with Alice," he said. And suddenly it struck us that being seen leading a goat up Glastonbury Tor on the night of a full moon might be the kind of activity a local policeman would be pleased to investigate. Glastonbury is full of nice Tea Shoppes with notices in their windows saying No Hippies Allowed. We shot down over the darkened bumps and tussocks at tremendous speed.

"All right now?" beamed Alice as we scrambled aboard. "I *have* had a nice day."

October passed and November was half done before either goat gave any sign of coming into season again, although they normally show at punctual three-week intervals.

I was not going to be thwarted a second time. I had found

a billy closer to hand and arranged in advance that the moment the crucial hour struck, we would arrive. Naturally, when Twitch signalled by a plaintive moaning that her time had come, it was a grossly inconvenient moment. It was a morning when there were visitors to be breakfasted, a morning I had set aside to prepare a talk for the local girls' school to be delivered later that afternoon. But there was no margin for delay. I shovelled Twitch into the passenger seat of the car and set off at fifty miles an hour for the Yarlington billy.

The Yarlington billy differed in many striking respects from the Glastonbury billy. He was not a diffident animal. Indeed, he shot forth from his shed like a cannonball dragging his owner behind him. Irritated by the hindrance of his owner (a gently-spoken man with an inexplicable affection for this sterterous, evil-smelling beast), the billy tried to kill him or at worst, emasculate him with some well-aimed butts. Fortunately he was distracted by my nanny's pleasing scents and rushed at Twitch with a lubricious smacking of lips. As he inspected her fore, aft and underneath he gave softly singing sounds of anticipation. While the billy owner and I stood there hanging on to our enraptured goats, I attempted a little conversation.

"What actually *happens* . . . ?"

"You get three goes for a pound." The owner doubled up and gasped as his billy made a sudden sidelong attempt to get rid of him.

"Three *goes* . . . ?"

Out of the corner of my eye I saw a brown blur.

"That's one. Two to go."

"*That's* one?" I echoed, impressed by the swiftness of the act. The smell was terrible. Again, the billy began smacking his lips and purring. Twitch, too, looked well satisfied.

"That's two," recorded and the billy owner as a further almighty leap was concluded and the billy's head was raised in a long, shuddering groan. "He'll get a bit crafty now," the billy owner warned. "He knows he'll be put away after the third go so he messes about."

We waited and chatted between dodges. With obvious

119

reluctance (though without any actual physical difficulty) the Yarlington billy finally performed his poundsworth and, fighting every inch of the way, was returned to his shed. We stood on the lawn talking of this and that while the musty stench of goat tangibly sank through my skin when quite suddenly, like one of Buster Keaton's buildings, the billy's shed exploded, all four sides and the roof flying in the air.

I dropped my goat and ran for cover as the raging, yellow-eyed beast returned for more.

Back in the car, I lowered all windows and gasped for breath as we drove hurriedly home. Twitch leaned her head out contentedly, appearing to smile at startled passers-by.

I turned her out into the field and raced to wash the car, my clothes, my hair. Behind me I heard that unmistakable throaty blare and ran outside again to find that Athene, nose pointed blissfully in the wake of Twitch, was so moved by the odour, she too had come into season.

"I thought you might be back," said the Yarlington billy owner calmly going to fetch his foul and much-loved beast.

That afternoon, drenched in *Madame Rochas*, I advised the local Sixth Form girls not to succumb too readily to the stereo-typed rôles of their sex, but to prepare themselves as capable individuals before rushing into marriage and motherhood. On the other hand, I warned, aware that my jumper carried a residual, richer scent than *Madame Rochas*, don't be over-eager to swallow the claims that there is no significant differ-ence between the male and the female of the species.

Five months to the very day, and a year after the birth of Narcissus, in an orchard scattered with fallen apple blossom, Athene gave birth to one billy and one nanny kid. Twitch, whose delivery I watched from my office window, gave birth to a single billy.

It was an astonishingly uncomplicated business. She lay on her side straining and groaning for a while and then, seemingly bored by the effort, rose, nibbled a solitary yellow dandelion head and again lay down to deliver her kid with a single, determined push. It slithered forth, clothed in a brown caul, followed quickly by the afterbirth. Busily Twitch set about cleaning her baby and when that task was completed, ate the afterbirth until not a trace of it was left behind on the grass.

Initially, milking the goats proved far more troublesome than milking a cow. They are nimble creatures, well able to leap from one's grasp.

I managed ultimately, by weighing each end of the goat down with one of my children, but even so, Athene contrived to jump on top of my head and left me squeezing teats that dangled over my nose. John solved the problem by building a small platform of bricks in the corner of the back porch, cementing them over and rigging a wooden guillotine structure at one end. As the goat puts her head through the gap to feed from a trough on the other side, you slam the hinged wooden clamp over her neck and prevent her retreat. It works beautifully.

With the frightful necessities done and the billies disposed of, we were left with one engaging nanny kid, who, robbed of her younger fellows perhaps, attached herself to Muffin and went for long walks with him through the surrounding meadows. His unathletic yellow back could frequently be seen parting grasses that shone with upturned buttercups, while behind him sprang a small white dolphin, the nanny kid, her head distinguished by two black circles, like spectacles, where the bud-like horns had been burned off.

In the first few months, as the goats tore at the new dense grass and the opulent hedges and their bags swung, peachy coloured, close to the ground, we averaged over three gallons of milk a day from the two of them. John began to look on the goats with more favour. They discovered that it was not a simple matter to leap barbed wire with a heavy udder.

I began a small milk delivery and sold my eggs. There was

too, the last of the broccoli, the first of the broad beans, the potatoes spreading their nice foliage down line after line in the vegetable patch, the honey that was to come, the cider that was to be made later that year from the small green apples formed in June – slowly as we harvested and prepared them we began to be effective and practical. From now on we expected the comedies and the tragedies to be smaller; we thought they would be more infrequently spaced than they had been in the first three years.

15

IT TOOK WEEKS AND WEEKS OF HUNTING THROUGH THE SMALL
ads in the *Western Gazette* to find a Rhode Island cockerel
for my small flock of hens – they numbered then, I think,
about a dozen brown layers, two bantam hens and, of course,
the two fine Silkie cockerels Solo had reared . . . They behaved like small, self-inflated generals, making much of their
ceremonial dress to impress a sense of their leadership on the
larger hens who responded to the puffing and strutting with
the kind of indifference that provoked absurd bouts of crowing from the muck heap. As it was, every time they leapt on
one of the larger hens, the Silkie cockerels fell off, but I
didn't anyway want to rear bantam crosses which lay poorly
and often look misbegotten.

We heard of a woman living on the Dorset border who had

some Rhode Island cockerels. So, first packing Daniel off to his cub camp which, rather disappointingly, was in the field beside our back paddock, we unearthed a cat basket and set off to pick ourselves a cockerel.

There were more than I could count. Hens and cockerels mingled in a clucking unruly mass in the backyard of a bungalow with inexplicably boarded up windows. The whole place seemed to have been taken over by poultry. Their owner was an East End woman who had come to live in the country and gone in for hens. "They just seemed to grow," she explained over the sound of the cricket match on television which the rest of her family stolidly watched in their boarded-up front room.

Every door she opened released another flurry of hens and chicks, even in the kitchen. Outside the yard was baked and bare with their scratching.

"Which do you fancy?" she wondered, chasing some pullets into the coal shed.

We decided on a fine young bird with a chestnut swathe of feathers cast round his neck like a Cossack cloak and an iridescent black cascade of tail plumage. "Right-i-ho," she said and called her husband to help catch him.

In the end there were five of us leaping fruitlessly at the air, crawling under their caravan and hurling ourselves full length on the hard, yellow ground. By the time the cockerel was eventually captured, crammed in the cat basket and driven home in the boot of the car, he was in a state of nervous shock and no longer looked the prepossessing bird we had chosen. His comb was drained of colour and his tail was reduced to a single black feather. We shut him in the hen house hoping that the scents of the harem would seduce him and stiffen his resolve to stay. At dusk, when the door had to be opened to admit all the hens who fluttered upward on to their perches, the cockerel shrank in a corner and chattered with fright: the sight of so many women advancing seemed to make him swoon with horror.

"Ah, well," I sighed philosophically, "perhaps it means he'll

124

be better tempered than the last one." And later that night I went out to lift the hapless bird on to a perch.

Somehow, on that moonless and leaf-surrounded night, the cockerel managed to escape. I could hear him crashing about in the branches of the walnut tree that overhangs the hen house but I couldn't see a thing. An earnest search was begun by John but not joined by me. Either I was very keen to get to bed or two glasses of wine with my supper had made me phlegmatic. All would be well, I assured my husband. The cockerel wouldn't stray far from the hens. Up in the branches he would be safe from the fox. First thing in the morning we'd find him, I yawned.

First thing in the morning I woke and felt guiltily ashamed about the false confidence I'd expressed the preceding night. Crawling quietly out of bed I crept out into a gleaming, dewy morning still wearing my nightdress and searched pointlessly about. Nothing. The wretched bird was nowhere to be seen. How could I have been so certain that his crowing would stake his whereabouts? My tennis shoes grew slimy inside, my nightdress was drenched, as I trailed back and forth through the grass gazing up into the thick leaves of the apple trees. Once more I trudged the length of the paddock uttering homely clucks. Passing the field shelter where the boys had built a wonderfully complex maze and den out of chicken wire and old hay (you crawled in at the side and wound your way round and round until you reached a central chamber), I sensed a stirring. Once more I clucked encouragement. Out of the middle of the primitive dome (it resembled a Mycenaean bee-hive tomb) an uncertain crowing arose. I ran to wake John.

"In the maze!" I panted. "Quick!"

Selfishly unwilling to crawl into the maze in a nightdress, I waited outside while John dropped to his hands and knees. As his rear disappeared into the entrance, the cockerel shot out of the top of the dome with an elongated squawk and fled on speedily rocking legs towards the thick hedge and six-foot drop that divided our paddock from the cub camp.

I too, began to run. Then, imagining Daniel's response to

his mother bursting through the hedge in a wet, transparent nightdress, I turned and ran the other way to fetch a dressing gown. John passed me as he went in grim pursuit of the cockerel, his hair bristling with coarse hay. He hurtled into the hedge, stopped and very slowly retreated backwards as if he were on a piece of film being re-wound to edit. "They're in the middle of prayers!" he hissed having glimpsed the cubs, our son among them, ranged in a respectful line. As it turned out, it was kit inspection. Even so, the disarray could have been enormous.

"Get them to help!" I hissed back and ran to find something decent to wear.

John, I am told, leapt into the hedge, startled the concealed cockerel and scattered cub scouts in every direction.

"Oh hello, Daddy," said Daniel as his father and a mass of screaming feathers broke through the inspection line.

By the time I returned Akela had summoned every cub available to capture and return the cockerel. I could see them spread out in a ragged line, headed by John, toiling up Charley Hill towards Brick Kiln. In quite the wrong direction. As they headed west, I spied the cockerel, a streak of chestnut on yellow legs, scorch across Joss Edwin's field and take a northerly dive through the hedge downhill through the fields that go towards Ladywell and Coombe Farm.

Hollering my discovery, I set off and bounced downhill between skittish heifers, keeping the bird in vision. He plunged into a blackberry thicket densely criss-crossed with briars over a width of some ten feet, so tangled that although I knew he was in there I couldn't see him at all.

The others came stumbling downhill towards me and gazed dismally at the blackberry patch. Gossamer, sheeting down the hill behind, suddenly caught the early sun, and glittered above us.

"There's nothing for it," I said. "You'll have to go in there."

The cubs encircling the blackberry patch, agreed. They all looked at John. "Yes," they said. "Mmm. You will." Daniel was silently hoping his father wouldn't let him down at this important moment.

"Here goes."

It took courage. It is impossible to advance into a black-berry patch ten feet wide and twelve feet high without having all your exposed flesh ripped. Ultimately, you become suspended by your hair and must be prepared to lose a considerable amount of it if you are to achieve your object . . . this, in a man close enough to forty to fight for the halt of a receding hairline, is as noble a piece of behaviour as anything I've ever witnessed.

So, the cockerel was retrieved. He spent four days huddled in the corner of the shed while his comb turned almost white from loss of blood, or nerve perhaps, and then recovered his spirits. He ventured out. He escorted his hens with growing charm and confidence. Possibly, the terrible frights he'd suffered at our hands from the outset discouraged him from ever attempting to make any attack on us, but I think not. I think he was quite naturally a gentle and a courteous bird for all the increase in the size and splendour of his appearance that took place in the succeeding months. On discovering seeds or grubs the hens had missed, he warbled an excited invitation to them to run and share his findings. Cockerels commonly do this, of course, to attract hens nearer to hand and, having lured them there, leap upon their backs. But my handsome Rhode Island made a genuine division of his feast. Copulation, which he was rather late mastering, he reserved for the moment when they were let out in the morning. Last hen out copped it.

In mid-October, Solo fluffed her small golden form over somebody else's eggs for three weeks surviving on a peck of grain, a sip of water, and successfully hatched out the first four Rhode Island chicks. In no time, it seemed, the leggy creatures lost their down and outstripped their small attentive mother in size, looking quite foolish as they ran to her for comfort when something untoward occurred.

She weaned them with great care. As the mild winter months drew on I watched her conceal herself in the bare

127

and slender clumps of hazel, observing her offspring from a distance. When one was momentarily separated from the others and ran about in a frenzy of alarm, she ventured out of her hiding place and led it back towards its siblings, then again sank into the place where her own black patterning merged into shadow and watched them forage for themselves with her round, unblinking eye.

16

WHEN AT LENGTH THE THIN, STICKY, GOLDEN TWIST OF honey poured from the extractor into one jar after another, I was pleased to have bees.

Three years were to pass before this aromatic ceremony took place in a hot kitchen, watched by people who had whirled the honeycombed frames in the extractor for some hours and shone with sweat.

The first year, nothing at all had happened. Because John was away at the critical time, the bees had either eaten their own store of honey or been robbed. The second year, because John was away at the critical time, wasps had invaded the hive, eaten the honey and murdered the bees. In the third year, they gave us forty pounds of clover honey. By most bee-keepers' standards, a modest amount. To us a store.

I feel divided about bees as John feels divided about goats. Just as the goats are my responsibility, so the bees are his. Just as I seem always to be absent when the goats ravage the cabbages or young balsam poplars, so John is rarely available when his bees swarm or require some other crucial attention.

Our failure (I use the plural pronoun with a sense of generosity) to do the right thing at the right time where the bees are concerned has been all the more embarrassing for being known about by the bee-master, Charles Oliver. Only one of the five bee-hives in our orchard was ours originally. The others belong to the BBC (the initals refer to the local bee-keeping co-operative) which is run by Charles, a likeable and immensely enthusiastic man, a retired high-ranking RAF officer who organises boys from the local public school into bee-keeping activities all over the town. Most of their hives are kept in other people's gardens. Wisely. Shortly after we arrived, Charles, having keenly noted our apple blossom, our abundance of clover, our unconstrained variety of wild flowers, suggested that bees might interest us. The hives arrived quite soon after the suggestion was made, followed by Charles, and a troop of boys all garbed in bulky protective clothing and square, mesh-fronted bee hats, who became frequent callers to the orchard. Although the clothing is deceptive and the modern bee-veil an ugly, obscuring, uniform object, it didn't escape my notice that the boys seemed to vary with each visit, and it crossed my mind that their interest in the hobby was decidely less pronounced than that of Charles. His dedication is beyond question.

Although he manages to spend surprising amounts of his time climbing the world's high mountains or living in kibbutzim and travelling around Israel on a bicycle, this retired grandfather never fails to attend to his bees' needs. It is quite shaming.

As a matter of fact, bees *do* interest me in a theoretical manner. I don't enjoy them tangling in my hair or roaming about inside my ear with a horribly amplified buzz, but their unique scheme of life fascinates me. Theirs is a society run for and by the women, a society in which the men, the derisory drones, are reduced to sex objects. It is a nice reversal of human life and I enjoy the conceit it represents, although I have no desire to see it exactly reproduced between our sexes. The drones leave the hive only once, to pursue the queen on her wedding flight: that is their sole purpose. They don't even possess a sting to defend the hive. Apart from that one sexual (and for most of them, unsatisfactory) outing, their life is spent crawling around the hive, where they are fed and tolerated by the female worker bees until their sexual usefulness is exhausted. As winter draws near and the hard season's store of honey is capped, rather than have the idle drones consume it, the workers shove them out of the hive to starve and die. A far remove from the tender services women traditionally perform, but very contemporary.

On the whole, though, I admire the female bee. She's hard working, scrupulously clean and selfless in her defence of the hive. Just as it moves me to know that a weed, once uprooted, still struggles to accelerate in its last moments towards the stage of seeding to ensure the propagation of its species, so I'm moved by the way a bee will sting the human who invades her hive, even though she dies as the barb is ripped from her own body. I don't dwell much on this wonder when the sting has been lodged in my flesh, I have to confess. As I say, I'm divided about bees.

Even their 'political' arrangement has attractive and repulsive elements almost equally mixed. The hive is close to socialist perfection, an altruistic submission of the individual to the state and it exhibits the very ruthlessness which makes that political possibility so open to question.

Work is organised with interesting flexibility. One bee in her lifetime will perform many different tasks but all her efforts are selflessly devoted to the corporate well-being of the hive. She raises another's children, she makes honey for the general survival, she grooms and feeds her queen not because the queen is powerful in any 'constitutional' sense, but because the queen is the sole layer of eggs: the source of the

131

hive's continuance. Only so long as it is in the hive's surviving interest is assiduous attention shown to her. Once age weakens her, the workers will abandon, even kill, her.

This combination of corporate purpose and individual unfeeling haunts me. But another image of the hive obsesses me even more and that is the unseen rule of this effective, hard-working, altruistic female colony by a single, masked human male – and it is preponderantly male rule. There are relatively few women apiarists. That arrangement too, has it reverberation in our larger world.

The bee cannot be controlled as a horse or a dog is controlled, it cannot be called or soothed or lured out of its own tightly regulated realm and made directly to serve a human purpose. The control has to be more subtle than that, more insiduous. Behind his mask, the apiarist has to devise conditions that will persuade the hive 'mind' towards a particular course of action, normally one that is in their own survival interest. Periodically the colony will swarm. Sometimes because they need more room or because perhaps they want to revert to the wild – nobody quite knows all the reasons – but unless the bee-keeper wants an extra swarm to increase his hives, swarming is a nuisance both to the person whose job is to collect the swarm and even more, to those whose garden has been selected as a likely place by the bees. So the bee-keeper must inhibit the urge. The man who clips his queen's wings is frowned upon. The method is too clumsily direct. It is better approved to cut out surplus queen or drone cells to discourage swarming for reasons of population pressure. But however good or sensitive a bee-keeper may be, the colony will still find ways of thwarting his stratagems. I like this determined ingenuity: it speaks well of the bee. Of female resilience.

I am tempted to think that the colony reserves its finer cunning for a particular kind of bee-keeper. Some are not very good – not simply careless or forgetful, as we are, on the contrary they're often the most punctilious of people – but they are rough. They remove sections and handle frames with a despotic brusqueness, as if angering the bee was a unimportant matter, as if being stung was a trivial and occupational hazard in the course of their honey-robbing. I have seen other men remove frames with their bare hands and turn them gently round while they describe this process or that characteristic, untroubled by the bees which crawl enquiringly over their hands with a sustained but steady motor buzz. The buzzing of angry bees is a shriller note altogether. John says they even smell quite different when they're enraged.

Because as I've said, John – through no fault of his own – has often failed to be about at the critical moment, I've many times been alerted by (occasionally steely-voiced) neighbours to the presence of a swarm in their garden. I used, politely, to go and look at the swarm, wonder at its size and spectacle, soothe the invaded household with the belief that swarming bees are quite harmless since they are glutted and soporific with honey and then race off to ring Charles for help. Some swarms I've simply allowed to go free since there was no hive prepared for them. One swarm was collected by a man who came all the way from Weston-super-Mare with a skep. Technically, after twenty-four hours, the owner of the land where the swarm has settled can claim ownership of the swarm too, but few bother. Some swarms I have firmly declared to belong to other people though it's frankly rather hard to recognise one's own bees, and another swarm, said to have settled under the floorboards of the chaplain's wife's bedroom, I simply didn't hear about until it was too late.

The Templars, who live in the mill cottage that spans the stream below us, have suffered more than anybody else from our bees. Their patience has been monumental. One Sunday afternoon last summer, when they called me to inspect a glimmering dark bronze sack of bees suspended from a branch directly above their two deck chairs, I felt I couldn't subject either them or Charles to my incompetence any longer and I must learn to take a swarm myself. Charles, overjoyed to find a genuine volunteer, showed me how.

Collecting a swarm is really quite easy, a delightfully impressive thing to do in front of an audience crouched behind flowering shrubs or closed bedroom windows. The truly confident collector, like Charles, doesn't even bother to wear a veil or gloves, but simply comes and raps the branch where the swarm is hanging very vigorously until it drops into the skep (or cardboard box) beneath. Charles then walks off with it once he's sure the queen is inside, for then all the stragglers will follow, puts it on the back seat of his car and drives home with bees zithering round his head. A more cautious collector will wear protective clothes, and position his upturned skep in a shady place, with one edge raised on a brick to allow all the dawdlers to find their way inside before removing the lot later in the evening, when the bees have settled and are more tractable. It's as well to smear the inside of the skep with honey in case you have, by some mishap, collected a hungry swarm which doesn't even belong to you. A hungry bee is an exceptionally ferocious bee.

Moved, I think, by my enthusiasm, Charles returned the following day with a new troop of schoolboys and his precious RAF flying suit for me to wear during a routine inspection of the hives. It was an honour to be allowed to wear the flying suit.

I completed my dressing with wellingtons, a square, wooden-framed 'veil' fixed over a crash hat and a pair of pink, kitchen rubber gloves. The boys had evident difficulty in restraining their mirth when I re-appeared. It is hard to maintain one's dignity in bee-keeping clothes.

"Got your dinghy-jabber there!" Charles looked at my lower right leg.

"My dinghy-jabber?" Following his gaze, I too looked at my lower right leg.

Charles bent down and seized a small, sharp, triangular-bladed knife, from a pocket in my drooping leg.

"What on earth is a dinghy-jabber for?" I enquired, eager to learn all that I needed to know about bee-keeping.

"For jabbing your dinghy of course," sighed Charles, wondering if he hadn't recruited a fool. From behind his own black mesh mask he explained that you had to sit on your dinghy in bomber aeroplanes and they had a terrible habit of inflating without warning, blowing right up between your legs and obscuring your view.

"So you jab them?"

"Exactly."

Relieved to discover the remoteness of the hazard, I stumbled hotly after the boys, who were still doubled up in unusual postures. If anybody sees us now, I reflected, they'll make a note of this sighting in their UFO notebook.

The hives, dull, vertical wooden boxes, like tower blocks for bees (the attractive, old-fashioned hive is no longer 'standard', of course, any more than the attractive old fashioned veils and wide-brimmed hats), were lifted open section by section. Bending to examine the unevenly-raised brownish honeycomb built up on the wax frames, I started as a series of vicious thuds struck my visor and an angry roar arose. The instinct to leap backwards and run is soon overcome when you realise the bees can't, in fact, pass through the mesh, but over-confidence is punishable. Unless you are completely sealed off at neck, wrist, waist and ankle, a bee will find its way inside your clothing and try to stop your gross thieving. Navy blue or rough woollen clothing I'm told, especially angers bees.

Although I have a very poorly developed fashion sense, bee-keeping clothes are hot and uncomfortable as well as ugly and because John has such difficulty preventing his glasses sliding down his nose underneath his box veil, I persuaded him to buy one of the more pleasing wide-brimmed hats with soft veiling draped from it. He first wore it the morning he went to check on a swarm he'd captured from the Templars' garden the day before (Mrs. Templar had been stung in the mouth, I'm ashamed to say) which had then been placed in one of his experimental Iron Age bee-hives: a clay-plastered wicker dome, especially designed for a film he was planning on Iron Age way of life.

Within ten minutes he staggered back into the kitchen swaying and moaning, accompanied by a hostile guard of

135

bees. An unusually aggressive strain – or perhaps indignant at the primitive living conditions they'd been offered – they'd been able to press right through the veil as the breeze blew it against John's skin and stung him liberally about the face. Many had crawled right underneath and, as John laid his head swooningly on the kitchen table, I picked bees out of his ears, neck, nose and mouth, leaving upright barbs in his flesh. Never have I seen such fearful stings. Never had I seen my husband – normally so tough I twit him about the rigidity of his upper lip – in such a dreadful fainting state. Terrified that he was about to pass out with pain, or worse – tales of people dying from allergic reactions to stings sprang into my mind – I doused his enlarged head with an anaesthetising spray I found. The cries redoubled. Now he began to cough, splutter, choke and stream from the eyes. I paused, put on my glasses and read the instructions on the spray. POISON, it said. For external use only, it said. Keep away from eyes and mouth.

Torn between swooning, suffocating and shrieking at me, John was fortunately too busy to die, but he didn't feel at all well. The inner membranes of his eyes, nose and mouth, foully inflamed, every joint and feature of his head curiously welded together in a single balloon, he very nearly lost interest in bees.

But we had just collected five pounds of early apple blossom honey, faintly greenish in colour, gorgeous in flavour. "Oh my darling," I wailed. "Here, have some of this! Honey is good for *everything*."

The following morning as I went down to feed the hens who live near the hives, Mr. Templar's face appeared through the hedge, one eye nastily swollen.

"Not the bees again!" I cried, aghast.

"No, not the bees this time, though one did sting me yesterday," he said almost apologetically, thus explaining his altered appearance. "No, it's not the *bees* ..."

"It's ... ?"

"I'm afraid your goats are eating my peas," he said.

17

THE TEMPLARS HAVE ENDURED A GOOD DEAL ONE WAY and another. Apart from the goats and the bees, they have to put up with the noise of the geese that are kept in yet another of our prolific rusting corrugated iron sheds in the same orchard as the bees. Mr. Templar swears he has never been woken in the middle of the night by the geese though I rather doubt him. He is nearer to them than we are and John is always springing out of bed in the middle of the night, pausing to clutch a gun and race after a fox that is never there. I think the geese give vent to a sudden, unexplained croaking in the small hours because one of them dreams badly. It takes only one to provoke all the rest into a mutual scraping cry. Foxes *have* been seen exploring the tumbledown hut for weaknesses. One has even pursued the geese across the lawn in the full light of day but none has ever been taken. The only goose we've ever lost went to a two-legged fox who, on the same night as he helped himself to our goose, dug up four potato plants on Mr. Crabbe's allotment. It was quite a feast he had before leaving town.

They mature into rather dense creatures, geese, but as goslings they outrival chicks for beauty. When I went to the Sherborne Castle farm to buy our first batch of day-old goslings, my breath was stopped in my chest by the sight of tray after tray of cheeping, vividly-coloured birds. Together, in so thick a crowd, their yellow and smoky down merges into a brilliant, almost lime-green moss, slashed by the orange of their beaks and feet.

At three to four months they have grown into large, white waddling creatures who move in a line of commonly agreed rank, upraised beaks searching out food, water or quarry, their orange-rimmed blue eyes flatly anxious.

Matthew says they remind him of housewives. They have all the pressure of middle-aged women heading for a bargain department – single-minded, but searching instinctively to either side as they advance, rudely driving all before them and expressing unreasonable indignation if any obstacle remains for a moment on their path.

Our first batch hunted Muffin off his guard territory at the top of the sloping lawn and, when he attempted to slink back, rose as one, heavy wings beating, hissing like steam engines and lunged forward to tug, ignominiously, at his tail. They can look very frightening indeed, especially when they take one of their blind runs at some object they dimly see approaching up the steep drive. For a moment, they fly, huge orange feet skimming above the ground, necks outstretched. But the proverbial "Boo!" is all that is needed to beat off a goose. If you stand up to them, as Muffin eventually and delightedly discovered, their corporate composure fragments into a silly female babble. White forms disperse like paper boats with a wind behind them.

Apart from their noise and their stupidity, ours couldn't even find their way back to their shed at night without being shown the way (I can only hope that Konrad Lonrenz's greylag geese are of a different intellectual order altogether, if I'm to respect the behavioural conclusions he draws from them) geese have two other drawbacks a potential owner may care to know about. One is that they drink vast quantities of water and if you don't live beside a river, you are obliged to carry buckets out to them all day long. The other is that although they do, unarguably, keep one's lawn a tidy length, they make it quite impossible to either sit or walk upon as they excrete their own body weight in the course of a day. All the same, they can be cheap to keep, and, if eaten 'green' (by six months old), make a very delicious, unfatty meal.

The first year we kept geese John took just one to the poultry market before Christmas but it managed to excrete so much dung in its paper sack that it fell out of the bottom and escaped across the car park. He brought it home and killed it himself. It's a man's task, breaking the neck of a goose. They are strong birds.

His first kill was witnessed by a vegetarian girl who lives in one of the cottages cresting the hill opposite. She cried all day. "How *could* you . . . ?" she wept. "They ran to greet you every morning."

The others he did more discreetly, albeit reluctantly. Holding them down to twist the neck is a horrible business, though relatively brief, but plucking them is a longer and frightful labour. Geese have two layers of feathers and if you don't start work on them while the bird is still warm, the second layer of down will defeat you utterly. John emerged from the corrugated iron hut four hours after he had entered it looking as though he'd aged forty-four years. His eyebrows, ears and hair were frosted white with down. After that, we sold as many as we were able to the butcher unplucked. It was worth two pounds off the price.

The second year we kept geese both our profits and losses were more dramatically experienced.

Firstly, we kept more geese, twelve in all. The increase in volume was so remarkable that a man living a mile away said he could hear them. Attempting to work through goose induced migraines, I felt I might more peaceably try writing novels in a disco.

Secondly, the summer was so unnaturally hot for our latitudes that the grass which sustains the geese simply perished and the birds turned grey with dust. It meant feeding them barley meal for months at five pounds a hundredweight. Plainly the fifty-pound profit we'd hoped to make on Christmas sales could be cut by half.

On the credit side, we'd become far more efficient at killing and plucking. Instead of ripping away for four hours at a bird with defiant rigor mortis, we found that by putting the dead bird between us in a tin bath continually filled with hot water and plucking together, we could do the job in half an hour. All the same we decided that we'd send seven birds to market and, ignorant of their destiny, they sat quietly side by side in the back of the car.

I dislike markets. I hate the way a man will prod a heifer round the ring to keep the bewildered creature moving. I hate the way they jab a pig to its feet or bash its snout if it looks threatening. I wasn't happy about the way our geese were slung upside down from the feet to be weighed, and noticed an RSPCA inspector trying to bandage the bleeding leg of somebody else's goose. If I am to be honest, though, I'm forced to admit that what made me angriest of all was the spectacle of the Ring – a group of three or four conspiratorial dealers – huddled together in a price-fixing brotherhood. The geese were selling for two or three pounds apiece unless a chance housewife peered in, spotted a promising bargain and made a bid. Immediately the price rose to six pounds a goose, then dropped again. One of ours sold at one pound fifty pence. It had cost me one pound at a day old. At that moment I felt and fully understood all the oppressed and exploited fury of a peasant farmer. Perhaps it was a salutary experience and in that sense a useful one. But I shan't keep geese again.

The other major noise nuisance is Nefertiti, the Anglo-Nubian goat. She too, is very stupid, though I can't perceive any clear relation between noise nuisance and brain size since my pigs, too, are shockingly noisy and yet highly intelligent. No, Nefertiti has all the nervy, squeaking mindlessness of the overbred pedigree animal (a characteristic observable occasionally in the human animal). She is the only one of my creatures I am sometimes tempted to kick out of sheer exasperation, but because all the other goats regard her hysterical response to any event with equal derision (to a large degree they provoke it by butting her whenever they can), I also feel a need to protect her. Once she has young of her own, I'm sure she'll settle down. Maternity appears to have a very sobering impact on most creatures. A kind of wisdom overcomes them.

Nefertiti arrived because my own kid (more accurately, Athene's kid) had been promised to the Holgates and I was so saddened to see her go that I withdrew immediately into the *Western Gazette* and answered an advert for Anglo-Nubian kids to console myself. There was a further, less frivolous reason. Anglo-Nubians, who are the most elegant of all goats, are also the Jersey cow equivalent of the goat world. They give a far higher proportion of cream in their milk and I was interested to see the difference for myself.

Since for my children it promised to be a fairly long and boring journey down to Dorset to look over the kids, I mollified them by promising that as soon as we had done business, we'd go on to explore Egdon Hill and eat our picnic there.

The road to the farm we were seeking wound uphill, narrowing all the way and threatening to vanish into heathland. A billy goat leapt out of the slender trees that grew beside the road and brushed against the Land Rover. Next, two peacocks flew across our path and we found ourselves in a bizarre yardful of goats, Pyrenean mountain dogs and Shetland ponies all of which their owner – a dour girl in jodhpurs – bred.

There was little exchange of conversation and I was disappointed to find that the only available goat was, like all my others, white, as Anglo-Nubians can have wonderful, onyx-like, marbled black and brown colouring. But colour was incidental. She had the long legs, the Roman nose, the large, pendulous ears of the breed. She was rather a good goat. (Plenty of bone.) But unlike mine, who came freely to be handled and to rub against you, who were led willingly enough and relished car-travel, this one took pop-eyed fright at everything and kept up a high-pitched, whining bleat.

We had to go up Egdon because I'd promised. Anyway, I very much wanted to see the high, bi-vallate fort that had formed so large and sombre a background to Hardy's novels. From the top, I told the children, we should be able to see the sea. Nefertiti kept up her silly, miserable clamour.

I found myself stuck (in a long skirt) halfway up a nearly sheer, thistle-strewn slab of Egdon clutching a tussock of grass in one hand while with the other I clung to a berserk goat, tugging against, fighting against her rope, attempting to pull me back downhill. I couldn't go down. Had I allowed the tension on her rope to slacken she would have had me rolling down some sixty feet of near-vertical stony ground.

The children stood at the top holding the picnic things, shouting encouragement, their hair blowing across their eyes.

We made it. And once we'd made it and I lay panting on the grass I realised that we could have come all the way to the top of this magnificent windswept hill by road like all the other tourists standing, shielding their eyes as they gazed out across small fields below them to the glassy sea below. I had imagined the place would be as forbidding and lonely as it was in *The Return of the Native* but I was wrong. Other walkers in stout shoes and khaki anoraks looked with disapproval at our flighty group (plastic bags, flapping skirts, troublesome goat and all), as they passed our tug of war. Since Nefertiti refused to follow anyone but (intermittently) Matthew, he volunteered to take her back down by the road and into the Land Rover. We watched him, her small white form trotting beside him with moderate willingness. We watched him open the driver's door, shovel her in, close the door and then, as he turned to come back towards us, we watched the passenger door fly open and Nefertiti leap out, straight up the fearsome rampart I'd previously scaled tus-

142

sock by tussock and away into a distant herd of cows who, alarmed by the unfamiliar creature in their midst, began to charge in untidy looping shapes further and further away towards the horizon.

From Liz, who once reared a herd of pedigree Anglo-Nubian goats, I've since learned they're all screwy, they all make this tormenting noise, none of them can be easily tethered and they throw a large proportion of hermaphrodite kids. Mine makes more noise than most since she appears to be in season all the time. We shall see.[1]

From another source I learn that we are doing profitable business exporting Anglo-Nubian kids to the Sudan which is a nice variation on fridges to Eskimos. Our most highly-prized Anglo-Nubian billy, recently flown out to Khartoum, stood at the top of the aircraft steps on arrival and dropped dead from the heat. It sounds in keeping.

[1] Eventually, after three fruitless visits to a fine Anglo-Nubian billy, it was discovered that Nefertiti was barren. Her continual bleating broadcast of 'in season' was, in fact, a sign that not all was well and by the time she was two and ready for mating, she had developed an ovarian cyst too substantial to be dispersed by powerful hormone injections. Anglo-Nubians often are sexually indeterminate. With hindsight, I wonder if the other goats' rejection of her wasn't prompted by their sense of her 'oddity' . . . March 1977.

18

"It's unbelievable," mused Liz, gazing at the hot, parched landscape, "but the cubbing season starts soon." She looked at me meaningfully.

After the burning summer of 1975 the countryside looked like the American prairie. Dry yellow stubble rose to an unbroken arc of blue. Only the occasional elm struck an odd and English note. Even more eerie were the skeletal black shapes of dead elms that stood like winter bones in the midst of summer.

"Heavens . . . Already?" I murmured. It was September and the corn was cut. Vast loads of perfect golden straw had swayed one behind the other down narrow lanes, scattering stalks on the bonnets of the cars behind. The purple leaves of the copper beech beside the house had deepened to a grape-like blackness in the sun.

"You'll be taking your mare at last?" Liz virtually stated.

"I'm not convinced she's totally sound," I demurred.

Charges of cowardice proclaimed themselves all over Liz's expressive face. "I've told you," she said, "she's bored, that's all. Once she sees hounds, she'll be a different animal, I promise you."

So I tried it. Just to see (you understand), if there *was* anything in what Liz said, to see if the faint, perhaps imagined lameness, *was*, as Taffy had believed, mere hypochondria left over from more punitive times. At six o'clock one cool morning we set out in characteristically plodding fashion to a meet in a village four miles away.

Some half a mile away from the village, the hunt lorry passed us and catching the babble of hounds inside, as it swung carefully round us, Bathsheba's sleepy head went up. Her pace quickened. She began to stride out in the wake of that exciting clangour.

Rounding the corner, we came within sight of horses and hounds clustering at the crossroads. Her highest expectations were fulfilled. Quivering, whinnying quietly within herself, she seized the bit more strongly and I found myself riding an unrecognisable animal. The old dream inside my head broke out of the skull's envelope – she became silky, springy, responsive, just trembling on the edge of an obedience that could be ruptured at any moment by a joyous burst of speed. The line between my hand and her mouth became vibrant, highly-tuned. Instead of driving her on, I had to restrain her under me. It was like holding back a coiled spring.

I was desperately proud of her. Excitement changed her entire appearance. Her great quarters were bunched beneath her. Her neck curved. Her intelligent head quickened and refined as eye, ear and nostril were extended to absorb everything that moved about her. Looking like an animal on a pre-Renaissance frieze, she drew forth admiring comment from one or two onlookers as she danced beneath me.

145

The first half hour of waiting round a field of kale was unbearable. While all the other horses stood as quiet and still as statuary in a formal garden, Bathsheba pounded the ground with a foreleg, ran back, plunged forward, then, thwarted, performed a rubbery rise and fall on the spot.

A surge of movement some yards away to our right and she was off, cantering past more orderly horses along the roadside verge and pulling hard. I began to realise just how strong she was.

As a gateway loomed, her ancient panic took over and she bolted through, barging other horses aside. Yelling apologies over my shoulder (for manners are insisted upon in the hunting field), we flew over the stubble at a pace that brought tears to my eyes. Beneath us, the earth was full of a seismic thunder.

Nearing the head of the field, another and narrower gateway forced a pause as horses and riders were reining back to pass through the gap singly. The waiting, the fear of a restricted space inflamed the mare's impatience. After being circled twice to calm her until her turn came, she tore the reins from my grasp, soared curiously through the air, slewing and bucking as she landed, hurled me to the ground and, galloping over me, sped riderless through the gate and disappeared.

There was no time for humiliation. Somebody, a field away, kindly caught my horse for me and I re-mounted to enjoy another half hour of undirected (as far as I could tell) chase through farmyard and plough. I saw neither hounds nor fox nor cub which didn't help me shape any informed opinion on the issue of hunting but Liz had made her point about Bathsheba.

I rode home on a mare that had blossomed out of an old and dust-laden fantasy. The wider questions of hunting, the fact that I had fallen off yet again, all these things (for the moment), dropped out of my mind as stones fall through water. We rode homeward up the steep incline to Creech Hill, its stegosaurian shape dominating the surrounding countryside and my spirits rose shamelessly with every stride. The sun climbed with us, shining through the knot of dead trees on the top of Trendle Hill opposite, down across the wide valley we had galloped that morning. All the little rivers glittered.

As November and the hunting season proper approached, the whole vexed question lay, a lump of undigested matter in my stomach. Since cubbing costs nothing and you don't have to pay a subscription (then fifty pounds for a full season) until November, I still had a few weeks in which to make up my mind. Writing a cheque would commit me. I couldn't afford it. I couldn't spare the time. The dithering inner argument went feebly on while I had Bathsheba clipped out in readiness and exercised her regularly. I disapproved. (Did I? Truly?). I was scared. (I'd seen some of the hedges one was expected to jump out hunting.)

Bathsheba and I practised jumping. We went over the cross country course at the Bath and West showground and she was so good, she was made lead horse to encourage the others. While out for a ride, we jumped everything in sight, including (with doubtful right) a five-barred gate that had been improperly padlocked across a bridle path. Swaying at the last moment to dodge a low bough, I unbalanced her and she crashed through it. I fell off on my head and she tore her fetlock. Marooned in a field she couldn't get out of I ran a mile to fetch the vet who came and stitched her up on the spot and unpicked the padlock. She was laid off for two months.

Destiny, I began to feel, was resolving this argument for me.

Shortly before Christmas I was able to start riding her again but perhaps because the weather was colder, it seemed to me that the stiffness had returned to her shoulders. She shuffled downhill like an old woman and relapsed once more into a dull and spiritless obedience.

This time the vet recommended Phenylbutazone, a pow-

147

der commonly taken to ease mild arthritic conditions. It was, as I understood it, comparable to a human being taking aspirin to reduce rheumatic inflammation, nothing more serious than that. Simply a drug that lessened pain and gave a large number of horses a considerably more enjoyable working life than they would have had without it. I agreed to try it.

The effect after ten days was dramatic. Bathsheba came out of her stable with a keenness that the weeks of rest had eroded. She moved more freely, jogging down the road in evident hope of finding hounds at the end of it. As the days passed and no such excitement greeted her, she settled once again into her steady, resigned lope. The fire that I had on that single day discovered in her, burned down.

'You can hunt her *now*," repeated Hugh irritably, then added more helpfully, "You'd get a reduced subscription for a short season."

"I'm still not sure she's absolutely right," I said.

"Of course, she is. Nothing wrong with her at all." And to demonstrate the truth of his judgment, he clambered on her himself and drove her round in a few ragged circles. "Nothing wrong with her whatever!" he called as he dismounted and slapped her neck. "Thoroughly good mare."

Another huge and boisterous family Christmas came. The goose was perfect, the general humour high but by New Year's Eve I was too exhausted to face another party and, leaving the others to their celebrations, went to bed before midnight.

Waking early in the pitch blackness I was dully conscious that, tired and busy as I'd been the night before, I had forgotten to shut up the hens. Pulling my anorak on over my nightdress I ran out into the darkness already in an agony of knowing what I would find.

Feathers carpeted the frosted ground. Everywhere. Everywhere I turned I found feathers that resolved themselves into brown, white, gold and iridescent shapes as dawn paled. It was a pearled morning of frost and mist. I walked slowly through it searching the ground, my footsteps muffled as though I were in a tall, enclosed, cathedral space. Everywhere. As far as I went – across the upper paddock, through the bare thorn hedge, all the way across the crusted slope of Charley Hill and down again, back through the lower paddock, the orchard, everywhere feathers scattered themselves in ugly fans. He'd taken every one of them: twenty-four in all. My gentlemanly cockerel, the white Babcocks, the brown layers, the young pullets we'd reared, the loyal little Silkie mothers. Solo.

As I walked round and round in desperate circles I wept bitterly for the loss of all my hens and the carelessness that had brought the loss about. The trail of feathers spread over half a mile. Instead of letting themselves be taken as hens usually do once they've roosted, they must have tried to flee. Two foxes at least must have worked together to remove so many corpses over so great a distance. Normally they leave a trail of headless birds behind.

"Happy New Year!" someone called across the valley as the mist lifted and the frost melted on the grass.

Matthew came out to feed his rabbits.

"Mummy!" he called in a loud whisper as he stood looking at their burrow-riddled run. "Look! They've got babies!"

Small forms vanished down the holes.

"They've had *babies*!" he repeated, his face alight.

At noon, after my parents had left for home (and generously given a cheque to help replace the hens), a single brown hen appeared walking cautiously out of the cover of the hazel clump.

She's called Odette. Three weeks later she survived another raid by the fox who left six corpses behind him that time. We have her still.[1]

[1] On 29th June, 1976, three days after writing this, a fox prised open the walls of the hen house – a vixen probably, with cubs to feed – and killed six hens, one of them Odette. In the same week it, or other foxes, made two visits to Jack Hopkins' place, taking over thirty hens and, levering the roof off their lovingly-made house, took one of Ted Hutton's prized pair of ornamental ducks, the female, whose first eggs were being incubated beneath her.

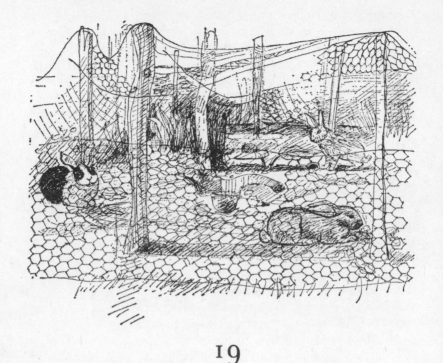

19

SENTIMENT MAY HAVE BEEN ONE OF THE CONSTITUENTS OF the sorrow I felt over the slaughter of my hens. I'd felt deep affection for them, certainly. But the regard I'd come to have for all my animals that grazed and pecked round Providence Place was a complex thing. While I don't believe I'd ever viewed them with the nursery affection that makes surrogates of animals, love-objects whose chief purpose is to give their owner a sense of being loved, my animals had, for nearly four years, been my closest companions and I owed all of them in different ways a very real gratitude.

Without them I could easily have sunk into lapses of self-pitying loneliness. My neighbours were kind, the place that I lived in beautiful. But I saw very little of John whose talk and support I value above anything and my children, lively and absorbing as they are, were either at school or, naturally enough, more disposed to enjoy the sort of games and jokes they could share with friends of their own age.

The animals stopped all the gaps. The dog was my attending shadow and, although it was a ruefully comic disappointment to me that I would never be the rider of my own generous imagination (like my singing, another feat I've always longed to do well, its outward performance was an infuriating mis-match of the pure execution in my head) it was still an intense pleasure to ride out against wind and rain and feel my little skill increase by tiny degrees, to sense the growing understanding between Bathsheba and myself.

The animals gave me more than companionship, however. They taught me an immense amount. In them I could watch a frankness of behaviour that simply wouldn't be possible in observing human beings. Well, it *would* be possible, but deviant. And in that respect they haven't made me withdraw from other people. Rather the reverse in fact: I feel I understand a good deal more about the fascinating oddity of human response. The sheer honesty and directness of animals (even their dislike of you) makes the tangle of human concealments exquisitely vivid.

Because of them I have gone without the new clothes, foreign holidays, restaurant meals and theatre outings I might otherwise have been better able and freer to enjoy but they've compensated that loss handsomely. They have been my theatre. They've been my entertainment and, like the best theatre, they've been a stimulus often forcing me to ask uncomfortable questions about human motivation that I would have preferred to avoid. My once fiercely-held feminist views, for example, have been considerably altered by perceiving the very real and highly functional differences between male and female animal behaviour. For all the variables of intelligence and cultural difference, there are still strands in our mutual animal behaviour that are simply wilful to ignore.

And there is another kind of gratitude that slips into the relationship you have with animals which are not strictly

151

pets. There exists between you a giving and receiving relationship that is quite outside the softer washes of affection. In return for my care the hens – not, of course, out of the goodness of their hearts – give me eggs. The exchange can be more fundamental than that. I have, as yet, shirked the task of killing one of my own animals but I have taken them to slaughter and I have eaten them. This pattern of things has a paradoxical effect – as the sentimental impulse to treat an animal as a human substitute recedes it is not indifference that increases (or so I have found) but the ability to admire and respect the animal in its own right. Possibly it is the same feeling that made the palaeolithic hunter draw his own image disproportionately small in relation to the bull or the deer he painted on the walls of caves so deep and inaccessible that it has to be assumed they had the most profound pyschological and religious significance.

I remember very closely an incident which made me distinguish between anthropomorphic love and proper respect for an animal.

One of the goats, Athene, fell ill. Normally, when the goats are put out in the morning or brought in to be milked at night, they travel in a column, running one after the other behind their 'leader'. Even if they've been tethered, the lead goat won't begin her run for home until every single goat is untethered, preferring to wait and browse until the train is complete. (To my amusement the three other goats will even wait for Nefertiti, if only to give her a sound bash before turning for home.)

On the evening in question, I went to unchain the goats hoping that the good clump of bramble and ivy I'd found for them would have helped Athene recover her listless appetite. It was dusk and as they ran down the hill ahead of me towards the gap in the hedge they use as a short cut to the stable I thought, in that deceptive light, that I was one goat short. It seemed improbable but I checked and found that indeed, Athene was missing. Climbing back up the hill again I found her making slow, unsteady progress down. The desertion of the others astonished me. But even after I'd guided her back to the stable, her body pressed against my legs for support, the others behaved as though she weren't there at all, bounding about in their customary pushy manner, stumbling over her, even treading on her in their anxiety to get at their food.

She, in the meantime, sat immobile, head raised, eyes half-closed. She knew that she was dying and awaited the event with a kind of grace.

Her tranquil acceptance amid the uncharacteristic brutality of the others was painfully moving and I sat down beside her in the straw to comfort her, very close to tears. She accepted my hand stroking her as unresponsively as she accepted the callousness of the other goats and the coming of her own death. She didn't avoid me but she didn't lay her head on my lap either. She simply waited in a contained manner for the inevitable.

Suddenly, as I sat there with tears streaming down my face I seemed to feel – very intensely – her situation as she herself felt it and I understood that by sitting there, fussing her (however unobtrusively), I was offending her animal dignity. That it was no part of her expectation to be loved unto death. That it was, conversely, part of her expectation to be left as the others had left her. I rose to my feet and walked away.

To conclude the story on a brisker and happier note, I went back and with John's help, pumped shots of Vitamin B into her atrophied thigh muscle to protect her liver in case she'd been poisoned. The treatment worked. But that doesn't alter my point. Medical treatment was necessary and effective. My emotional response was of no worth at all.

My emotions on that New Year's morning when I found the bodies of my hens strewn in wanton trails across the hillside included anger.

Had I been able to, had I been there, had I caught that fox slithering off with one of my hens in his jaws, I'd have done worse than hunt him. I would have torn him apart with my own hands. The desire for revenge burned that furiously, despite the fact it was I who had left the hen house door open. Culpability, I'm afraid, often enlarges the appetite for revenge.

"If you'd ever seen the destruction a fox leaves behind ... !"

I've heard that one many a time as a prelude to the case for hunting. It's not enough in itself to support the case, but it's not an empty point.

That fox's massacre wasn't the single dramatic incident that changed my views about hunting. The fox was only one factor and hunting only one part of the conclusion – albeit a fairly central one and, in a sense, an emblematic one – to a much larger, more general change of view that had gradually come about as the values and propositions of daily metropolitan life became less and less appropriate to the way I now lived. I was genuinely hurt and baffled when an acquaintance said I was becoming more Right wing because the change – when I stopped to consider what form it had taken – wasn't one that could be relevantly submitted to any political measurement. It was more in the nature of a cultural change, comparable to slow acclimatisation in a foreign country. I hadn't suddenly decided that flogging was a deterrent or that the nation was being sapped by scroungers. I didn't feel any need to establish my social status by mixing with the hunting 'set'. Indeed, I was far more of a manual labourer than my critic but it would have been tactless, perhaps, to point that out. It was undoubtedly true that my initial opposition to hunting had largely dissolved and, when charged with the abominable sin, I found it very hard to formulate any immediate intellectual reasons for the alteration. The change was part of a slow and diffused process that became much clearer to me with the arrival of the Scraggies.

We replaced the hens the fox had taken with a dozen Arbor Acres (which could be described as black hens although the blackness of their feathers is entirely composed of purple and green), some Rhode Island crosses and these fourteen pathetic objects John brought home in a sack from a local battery farm. They were going cheap and no wonder. A

sorrier collection of fowl I've never seen: they were so re-
volting it was quite a problem even to touch them.

Battery farms prefer to discard their poultry the moment
they go off maximum lay because it's more economic to
throw them out than wait for them to recover their vigour –
if indeed, these ever could. Looking at the debilitated birds
spilling out of the sack I thought the pot might be their
most merciful end and was rather tart about the fiver they'd
cost.

Their necks were a naked red where the feathers had fallen
(or been torn) out, similarly their behinds. Their combs were
bleached and withered, their feet a softened white and their
state of mind alternately catatonic and hysterical. Diagonals
of terror, they strained against a corner of their shed wailing
with fright, unable to perch. They neither knew how, nor
were their claws hard enough to do so. When we put them
out they showed no ability to scratch food for themselves
and squawked backwards with terror when food was thrown
to them. They ate nothing. They didn't even know day from
night and instead of instinctively roosting when dusk came
they crouched helplessly about in the orchard waiting to be
individually picked up and lifted onto a perch they promptly
fell off. Every natural instinct had been bred out of them.
They were designed for egg-laying and that one function
exhausted, they seemed destined to die.

Knowing nothing else, they'd doubtless been content and
efficient in their battery house. Their world as far as they
were aware was one in which manufactured food passed
beneath their beaks, piped water was released by pressing,
day was infinitely long because electric light was left on to
encourage steady laying and their droppings were no nuis-
once to them because they fell tidily away to be removed by
some other agent.

Suddenly exposed to air, rain, grass, grubs and the discomfort of sitting in their own faeces they sickened with
fear and starved. I was prepared to allow them as long as
eight weeks to see if they would recover their natural res-

155

ponses but it looked as though they would fade away before one week was up.

Like me, though more extravagantly so, they'd come from a streamlined, modern environment where every comfort was subtly provided and now, their support system abruptly withdrawn, they had no instinctual resources to fall back on. It was their inability to feed themselves which shocked me most profoundly. It had to be a desperate corruption to generate caducity of this order.

I was reminded of the little girl who had come to collect eggs with me one day and knelt down beside me as I fumbled under a hen in the nesting box. "Do eggs come out of hens' bottoms?" she'd asked with shocked repugnance as the connection impressed itself upon her, a repugnance only exceeded by her response to the sight of milk squirting from an udder. Not at all reassured by my straining the milk through muslin (admittedly the material collected a good few hairs and wisps of straw), she would have dehydrated rather than drink it.

I refuse to be drawn into the debate wherein I am expected to say that my milk is better than bottled milk, my eggs better than those with a lion stamped on them, my vegetables more rich in vitamins and flavour than the clean, plastic-wrapped variety of the supermarket. It may be true, it may not – it doesn't interest me. What *does* interest me is the vast gap that exists for most of us in this country today between the production and consumption of food. The complications of that detachment are vast.

Perhaps it begins with detachment from the nipple. Perhaps from that moment of rupture, the retreat from one's food source begins and with it, a retreat from any close awareness of one's true dependencies. In between the baby's mouth and the breast that is both his larder and his comfort seep the world's giddy distractions – its toys, its bells and books and trains and teachers, its host of faces, conflicting routes, its songs, its smells – all becoming the substance of successive days in which a mother or nameless canteen staff or a distant farmer or machine perhaps, quietly supply the

156

pap that frees us to confront the world's astonishing alternatives. Poverty and hunger prevented our ancestors enjoying much occupation beyond food gathering and preparing – except for a little ritual observance to propitiate those forces who might make the circumstances for food gathering and hunting more favourable. It prevents the Third World peasant still.

When food is plentifully available whatever the season, it is easy to forget that food *is* life. Had I spent these three and a half years in Calcutta or the Brazilian jungle, the lesson would have been vividly apparent to me within twenty-four hours. As it was, it took a little longer for me to realise how easy it becomes the simplest error – running a finger over tins on a shelf, snatching milk bottles off the doorstep before rushing for the early train, sloshing boiling water on a powder that instantly transforms itself into coffee or soup – to think of food as a domestic and secondary matter and to think life is primarily about political power or improved wages or David Bowie or measuring light waves or any of a thousand things that can't engage the interest until the belly's filled. Political principle *grows* from the belly, from the right to be free of need.

It's easy to forget because it *is* so large and simple a truism. Shovelling food into our mouths day after day, one imagines that only a fool *could* forget that food is breath. And so, because it's as obvious as the nose on one's face, it is forgotten – or taken for granted – and at that moment of forgetting we acquire the licence to a distorted view of ourselves. Looking at my animals – who could gorge themselves on one another but don't because my provision frees them of hunger – I sometimes wonder if it's food rather than morality that makes us tractable. Once fed, I'm at liberty to describe myself as peaceable and full of rectitude if I so wish, but take my plate away, face me with starvation and all the things that give me cause for self-congratulation are liable to evaporate. It may be absurd to think of civilisation as something built on mutton chops, spuds and flour. It's alarming too, because its frailty proclaims itself.

157

I suppose it was this simple relation of things that had slowly worked itself into the texture of my living and outlook as my daily routine had changed and the microcosmic gap between my own production and consumption of food grew smaller. All manner of little events and views were inconspicuously changed by it. The landscape was less charged by blind lyricism as I grew accustomed to Hugh's voice grumbling that a view is well enough but you can't live off it. "Your view is my bread and butter," he would say dourly, recalling all the calamities of weather that had befallen his farming.

Rain was no longer something that ruined a hair-do and required an umbrella (something everybody discovered during the drought). The frost that lay on the metal bolts I opened first thing on a dark morning – so cold it burnt my fingers – was a good and necessaiy thing. The killing of foxes wasn't quite the sport elegantly summarised by Wilde as the unspeakable in pursuit of the uneatable. Uneatable they may be, but foxes steal what we eat. Or to quote Hugh again, "They're vermin. Like rats but better looking. Don't suppose most people would think it unkind to kill the rats in their larder. Mind you," he added, "I like rats. Intelligent creatures. So," he mused, "are foxes." Thus the 'unfathomable' respect of the hunting man for his prey.

I had become altogether more familiar with death. It isn't a piece of artful conjunction on my part to note that on the very morning the hens were killed Mathew's rabbits revealed their young for the first time. It was true. Such a pattern is commonplace. Death is as fixed a component of the countryside as wind and weeds. Discovering nothing indecent in itself, it makes no attempt at concealment. If life is food, death, too, is food and the two poles are joined without the help of transcendental philosophies. Death is life: it is a witnessable fact. Even my cats and the fox I accuse of hooligan slaughter, who may well be killing more than they need, are not really amusing themselves with murder: they're keeping their necessary weapons sharp or – in the fox's case – providing for a poorer time. I have known a fox return on the night after his massacre to collect the corpses left behind

158

and bury them in a manure heap or stuff them down a rabbit hole. The prudence that is handmaiden to survival dictates the fox's seeming excess as irresistibly as it dictates my cutting more hay than will be needed for a normal winter's siege.

Death is the aphid I have just squashed on this page, it is the cutting of barley, it is the maggots my hens retrieve from the muck heap. It is the dropping of ripe plums or soil dried out by the sun. It is the lorry I can hear changing gear at the bottom of the hill while the cows inside moan on their way to market. It is an egg fallen from a thrush's nest or the snail I can hear that bird smash on its favourite stone. It is the web in the corner of my bedroom or my pig, pursued by the man in a blood-bright rubber apron.

On that day I called at the slaughterer's to collect our engaging Saddleback hog, now jointed and piled in plastic buckets, his tail and snout protruding from the soft heaps of flesh, I made myself eat part of him. I *am* a meat-eating parasitic, killing, territorial animal and I feel as great a need to face that fact and explore its contingencies, however distasteful, as I once felt a need to confront my female nature or as homosexuals and blacks may feel the need to explore the things that distinguish them in the human throng. Once, I sought out (and some days, still do) the distinctions that make me special and separate. Sometimes, I find resemblances more stunning. To be a black or gay or working class or a woman is to acclaim one facet of oneself as a human being. To face the broader case of being a human *animal* is more disturbing. It is a darker matter, often unrewarded with the raised esteem that springs from other self-defining explorations. On the contrary, its revelations are rather humbling and possibly require a masochistic honesty to confess to them at all but I know that if I make no acknowledgment of my simple animal conformities, the opportunity to deceive myself about my motives and thus arrive at hopelessly false solutions is substantially enlarged. Intelligence, like fire, is marvellous, powerful and potentially injurious. An instrument of truth and understanding and equally, an instrument of deception: the deception each one of us prac-

159

tices in relation to ourselves. At its meanest extreme it is the thing I use to conceal a base motive with a good argument, at its grandest, it is the thing that can present war as glorious, virtuous or necessary . . . For protecting others from perilous ideology, for bringing the people of poorer lands the benefit of our own wisdom and prosperity. Even when the cause of war is indisputably proper, we need a verbal surface, a stupendous rhetoric before we're ready to surrender our cherished intellectual and moral inhibitions about killing or territorial aggrandizement. And, quite often, underneath it all lies the old, unending need to eat.

Watching my animals I wonder *why*, why it is so hard for most of us to confess to the cluster of impulses generated by the fundamental animal needs of food and survival. Freud was considered to have made a most important contribution to human self-perception by unlocking one part of our unconscious motivation, but the factor he singled out – sex – isn't a *human* prerogative, though the distortion of its drive may well be.

Most of the instinctual driving forces (to do with aggression, territory, security, dominance, competition) are overlappingly bound up with sex, are shared by all animals including ourselves and are all linked to surviving on the available food supply. But we don't like calling this tangle of things our animal nature. We call it – if we admit to owning such drives at all – human psychology as though even our hang-ups were something above the animal realm. *Why?* A distinguished cleric once assured me most urgently that man is not an animal at all but something quite other. Of course, he and I are animals. To pretend anything else is a colossal prudery, or that's what I'm driven to conclude, since few people nowadays can share Darwin's horror over the implication of his evolutionary findings – the disintegration of the Creation story into impotent myth. And yet something of Darwin's appalled response remains. Are we back to the dog haters who are shocked by the sight of open, unashamed copulation and defecation not in the fields, where most decent animals do it, but in the High Street where humans

160

have to walk? Are we in the company of those who describe other people they judge unfit to be members of the human race as pigs, snakes, toads and asses?

In part, I think our peculiarly adamant dissociation with other animals is little more than superstition, a quite irrational feeling that if we own up to aggression for instance, we shall promptly become more aggressive. Certainly, being more frank about sex has made us more open in our sexual behaviour but that, on the whole, is considered a good thing. I don't imagine that identifying certain aspects of ourselves as 'animal' in the confused weave of behaviour will increase the possibility of our rampaging about in unfettered attack. We are percipient beings and, recognising that we are more aggressive than most animals, we are surely just as likely to recognise that we need whatever just and compassionate checks we can devise for ourselves in due proportion.

Still, the anxiety over being thought animal remains. It manifests itself in the fierceness of some intellectuals' attack on ethologists like Robert Ardrey, Konrad Lorenz and even, to a lesser degree, Desmond Morris. The fear that by relating animal behaviour to human behaviour one is led to adopt a savage, sometimes fascist viewpoint, is based on a rather mistaken view of animal nature. When my political critic rebuked me, he was implying that I was tumbling towards an embrace of the Right's natural order of excellence and deserting a Leftist belief on human perfectibility. That isn't at all where I stand. The most fervid believer in a natural order of excellence, a member of the National Front, say, would be more reluctant than most to own his relationship to the grunting ape. No, I believe I am animal, imperfect and perfectible. I do not believe the imperfect element necessarily derives from the animal element. Sometimes I think imperfection arises from rational thought based on dishonest or false premises. Someimes I think imperfection arises from a suppression of the animal element. Certainly I think that it is quite wrong to assume 'animal' means barbarous. In the hours I've spent watching both my animals and wilder creatures, too, I've come

161

to see that animal nature is neither as cruel, nor as hierarchic, nor as without 'moral' as it often supposed. The animal world is not designed as a vertical chain of tyrannies with man commanding the sovereign position. It is politically more subtle, circular and interwoven than that. It is a long, cyclical chain of relationships in which any one group becomes dominant at its own peril because it risks, thereby, destroying the very groups which lease it life. No creature holds the freehold on this planet: the dinosaurs proved that.

But as long as food is plentifully available animal crudities can be denied or suppressed or so re-directed in specifically human ways – shopping, moving to a bigger house, roaring for the local football team, sitting for an exam – that they cease to resemble animal activity at all. We muddle endearingly along, teaching our children that competition is foolish and unjust at school, but depending upon it in trade and diplomacy, rescuing people from territorially defined dwellings called slums and re-housing them in coops we are surprised to find desecrated. Never mind, it's our contradictions that make us interesting.

Although my cats torment their captive mice and Muffin will give vain chase to a hare exposed by the harvester, none of my animals (as I said earlier) prey on others that belong to the household. Although their territory is shared and although Tiger will leave in a short-lived sulk after a newcomer's arrival, they know that I, the welfare state, will provide all the food they need and it seems to inhibit their desire to gobble one another. There is one exception.

The unqualified wildness of Matthew's rabbits is so deeply bred that the restraints of our small civilised 'state' cease to operate where they are concerned. The rabbits themselves are oblivious to them and possibly their disregard for the rules in some ways identifies them as fair game.

We kept the doe and the buck in a good sized run with wire netting some six feet high surrounding them.

The five babies who had appeared on New Year's Day,

162

scuttled about the run growing plumper and less timid as the days passed. They attracted passionate attention – from neighbours' children, from Muffin who spent hours gazing at them through the wire and from Blot sitting equally absorbed, beside him. But when first one, then another baby rabbit disappeared, it was Aurora, who stalked all four sides of the run her green eyes hard with ravening, that I most suspected. I couldn't imagine how she was able to leap into the run. Even if she contrived to do it by climbing a neighbouring tree and pouncing down, I couldn't think how she found the leverage to spring out again. Then I saw her inside.

Another baby rabbit disappeared.

I found its small grey headless body on the lawn. Saying nothing of it to Matthew, I secretly took a friend's advice to shut the cat in a small space with the dead rabbit fastened round her neck. "That way," I was promised, "the smell'll sicken her for good."

When I secured baler twine round the rabbit's body and tied it firmly to Aurora's neck, shiny coils squelched out of it. I shut her in the small cobwebby greenhouse and peered in from time to time. Within four hours she'd worked it off. I re-fastened it. When I next looked in, she'd not only manoeuvred it off, she'd eaten every scrap of it.

"What we do with a dog that chases the hens," said Jack Hopkins, drawing on his pipe, "is tie the dog in the run for three days. I've never had one trouble the hens again after that."

There were two babies left. Confessing the truth to Matthew, I guiltily tied Aurora up in the sun and left her for the prescribed time. She used it well, familiarising herself with the rabbits' movements, allowing them to hop close to her unalarmed. As soon as I released her, they vanished.

In February, another litter of eight were born and found, some ten days old, dead in a cold damp hollow. They were packed as neat as sprats in a tin. I buried them. "*Next* time . . . I promised Matthew who looked tearful over their entombment in the compost heap. But the doe took us unawares and in late March, when the primroses still clustered on the bank behind the run, she gave birth to a third litter of eight. We thought them safe in a hutch placed within the run. It was fronted by a mesh coop the shape of a Toblerone which only the mother could wriggle through.

They grew. Singly they disappeared. I rescued one abandoned in a corner of the run and fed it on a dropper for a few days before returning it to the depleted litter. Aurora was nowhere to be seen those days.

As I mixed a mash for the pigs one morning, a terrible screaming ripped the air, I ran towards the rabbits in time to see a carrion crow lift itself up over the wire, a baby in its claws. My arrival made it drop the baby who seemed none the worse. The crow flapped and settled heavily on a fence post nearby awaiting a fresh opportunity.

We threw strawberry netting over the wire.

Three, four, five more went. One, a black one, remained.

"I hate Aurora!" said Matthew fiercely one night and flung her off his bed.

"It may not be her all the time," I said. "It could be a stoat . . ." (He slid down beneath his blankets, not listening.) ". . . or a badger even. Burrowing underneath. I'll look in the morning."

Later that night Matthew came downstairs. 'I can't sleep," he announced and watched television for a bit before going to fetch himself a drink from the kitchen. He came back into the room and stood in the doorway silent for a moment. Then his containment burst and a great sob broke out of him. "My rabbit . . . !" he wept.

Half a black baby rabbit lay on the hall floor.

Aurora crept out.

In June, two days before the now emaciated doe, her black coat bare where she'd torn out her nesting fluff, revealed her fourth litter, we had completely wired over the entire run. Nothing could get in. Five babies.

Then four, then three.

"There are only two babies left," murmured Matthew forlornly one morning after he'd come in from feeding them. He was beyond tears any longer.

The truth dawned.

"It's the buck then," said John, "I always thought it might be him as well." And the big white rabbit with lilac eyes was removed from the run. The two babies grew healthily.

That buck had plenty of room and plenty of food. There was no sensible reason for him to devour his children but his wildness, his instincts, were more pronounced than his appreciation of the welfare state. Of greater curiosity to me, was the behaviour of the doe. As far as I knew, she'd made no attempt to defend her offspring. Certainly she'd shown no sign at all of loss or distress when they vanished, as most other mother creatures do. I wondered if the legendary heritage of rabbits, the fearful capacity to overbreed, normally regulated by other predations in the wild, had built a compensatory indifference to motherhood into her. The threat of overcrowding possibly made it needful that she should be a bad mother.

Some of the questions the animals raise, are, as I said, uncomfortable. They rarely lead to clear answers, only speculation and I know the limitations of that. But the doe made me wonder.

I can see that in an overcrowded world it is conceivable that strongly-defined maternal responses and desires are potentially hazardous. Is there an element of this primeval consciousness at work in our changing female expectations, in our readiness to accept abortion (however sound the social arguments proffered), or is the change simply a surface matter of greater female economic independence, better education, better contraception? I'm inclined to suspect that all these things come together in a subtle evolutionary mesh, just as I'm inclined to suspect, watching a mother animal snap and strike out at her maturing young that the conflicting and rebellious phase of adolescence is a necessary as well as a painful thing: a hostile breaking of the bond both parties need to experience (often more marked in the parent, oddly) to pave the way for independent life. I've also been forced to ask myself whether the close attention of the animal parent for the very young isn't all the more necessary if the infant is to be sufficiently secure in itself to withstand the shock of 'adolescence' and not see it as one more stage in a continuing pattern of rejection that has always been present in the relationship and which the infant, having learned, will then enact in its turn.

I know now – too late – that you can't explain to a tiny child that your going out to work all day makes you a lovelier mother in the evening. All the child can grasp is that it does not, for reasons it cannot fathom, merit your total attention. I have watched rejected young animals grow into regressive, timid adults, hanging back from the main group, snatching fearfully at their food. Conversely, I've seen others with a more fundamentally assertive nature, become unsocial by virtue of their over-aggressiveness. Whichever way their infant rejection affects them, the two broad types resemble one another in their weakened ability to function co-operatively and I can't help reflecting that human survival is grounded in our co-operative nature, a quality so marked it has overcome our lack of natural body-weaponry. I also find it intensely engaging to wonder whether the hunting hypothesis developed by Robert Ardrey might be right – it's certainly plausible – and that all our 'virtues' of co-operation, altruism, quick-wittedness and courage grew out of our obligation to hunt and kill, that such qualities were indeed our weapons and that to view our development as one in which the growth of moral values restrained our bestial savagery is to regard the whole course of our development in a back to front manner.

More authoritative men and women than I can pick at one strand or another of his argument but taken as a whole, it remains persuasive. I can't pretend for one moment it was anything but primordial rage that made me want to hunt down the particular fox who took my fowls and left a sneer of feathers over the hillside, but when I consider the general question of hunting and the fact that I finally succumbed to its pull, Robert Ardrey's thesis helps confirm my sense that the chase is not quite the cruel, foolish, over-dressed and empty ritual it can appear to be.

Yes, I went. Perhaps I went because the animal in me had become more pronounced, I don't know. I could provide a rational case for hunting but then I would exemplify my own criticism of the intellect: using it to arrange a good argument around a selfish motive. I could say – and it wouldn't be entirely spurious – that I went in the spirit of scientific enquiry, to find out for myself what coloured and motivated the chase. If that were the claim then it proved to be a bitterly equivocal piece of research.

No. I went because I wanted to hunt. I wanted to hunt because my horse wanted to hunt more than anything else in the world. And horses have no moral scruples whatever on the matter.

20

Stasis in darkness.
Then the substanceless blue
Pour of tor and distances.

God's lioness,
How one we grow,
Pivot of heels and knees! – The furrow

Splits and passes, sister to
The brown arc
Of the neck I cannot catch.

IT AMUSES ME TO DISCOVER THAT SYLVIA PLATH WASN'T prompted to write this, the title poem of her collection *Ariel*, by a fine-limbed blood horse speeding at a blurring pace across the long curves of the West Country. Ariel, from all accounts (rather like Bathsheba), was docile and elderly. It doesn't matter. At some moment that creature – she and the horse together – must have been seized with the exultancy that comes in part from sheer speed, in part from fear, in part from a brief, flawless unity of horse and rider and the earth beneath and partly from the tearing of the wind as it resists your entry into its private element of air.

Like Bathsheba, Ariel may never have been very prepossessing in the conventional way of an Arab stallion, say: awesome to the most uncommitted eye. But the creature Sylvia Plath describes isn't wholly imaginary. The ordinary *can* be transformed at the point where the real, the imagined and unconscious meet. Their mutual collision creates a whirlpool that draws all three elements into its single, encircling movement.

To the outside observer who recalls an altogether duller collection of detail, the transmutation on paper may look absurd and I must truthfully admit that during those mild, end-of-season months, I spent far more time preparing my beloved, oddly-shaped Bathsheba for her outings – cleaning her, cleaning her tack, cleaning both again (of thick encrusted mud) on our return – than I ever spent hunting. I'm surprised when I look at my diary to see that we only went eight times in all, that some of those outings were no more than two hours long, that much of the time was passed standing hushed and still while hounds ran in bewildered, grumbling circles unable to discern any scent.

Those aren't the memories that remain uppermost in my mind. The prints that dominate are the ones where Bathsheba and I, weather and landscape, merge. I am, of course, kind to myself. I don't topple or waver or cringe and perhaps for ten seconds or so, I didn't. Those are the moments. Galloping stirrup to stirrup alongside others, breaking free and forging ahead to take, with a minimum of check, a gate so placed on the hillside that we seemed to leap into the blue bowl of an entire valley; being part of a body of horses wheeling suddenly as the line is unexpectedly found and surging together like an ocean breaker; crouching along the mare's damp neck as we wind down paths under low-hanging forest branches; the intermittent, sparking of hooves in the sun-spotted darkness : lapwings rising off the plough to one side of us, peeling away to expose white underbellies; peering through divots of flung mud hurled up by horses galloping flat out in front of us to fly a broad and racing winter brook – knowing, as we take to the air, that we will land together and safely; checking, in a crowd at a covert while the steam rises so thick from the animals' flanks we seem gathered in a weird secret fog of our own; the heart-stopping sight of the fox as he breaks from the spinney, a powerful streak of red-gold, narrowed from nose to brush by the length and speed of his movement; the crashing of water as a whole company rides boot-high through the river and bounds up the far bank, a seal-like succession of sleek quarters. Those are the images at the front of the eye. Behind, crowds a clumsier selection.

The solitary rider with boiling face whose legs flap away at a horse refusing to join its fellows on the far side of a fence and being loyally cheered as it finally clambers through : fiddling with the catch of a gate while the rest of the field waits impatiently behind me : twice sailing over a large hedge to see the scarlet coat of the Master crouching in the ditch beneath me and once seeing a woman impaled on a thick, thorn hedge unable to move or even to speak as the barbs hooked into her bottom : rain slamming a metal shutter down over the countryside and emptying itself into my collar and boots, turning the leather reins to ungraspable slime in my icy hands. Days when nothing happened at all beyond a little fruitless trotting round and round the same roads when concentration lapsed and gossip was the day's liveliest sport.

On the very first day I prepared to go out I was too nervous to have dared speak to anyone. There were several reasons for being nervous. The little bit of cubbing I had done did not, I knew, compare with hunting proper. It was a slow, ragged and rather casual business, cubbing. There was very

170

little jumping, few fast runs and you wore your ordinary 'ratcatcher' (that is, customary tweed jacket, polo neck and breeches) clothes.

Liz had tried to teach me the mysteries of stock-tying. At home, alone, I couldn't remember the sequence of threading and folding at all. The stock, originally sparkling white, grew grubbier and grubbier. The borrowed back stud slipped down my spine into my pants and I had to start all over again. By the time I had re-assembled myself I was late, hot and apprehensive.

Bathsheba, being grey, was not as clean as she should have been since she'd managed to lie in her droppings the night before just on a point of her quarters which were not quite covered by the rug. I tried wetting and scrubbing at the patch which only enlarged it. I'd attempted to plait her mane and given up since the few plaits I *had* completed lay in such irregular sausage-like order they didn't improve her appearance at all. I picked out her hooves and then oiled each one with a small paintbrush. It was difficult bending down with a tight stock round one's throat – the blood supply to the head felt cut off. I wondered whether all this formal ritual grooming of the horse and rider was of the least importance. The likelihood of being plastered in mud half an hour after the meet moved off was very high.

Hugh had said it was important. Every item of dress had its reason for being he'd told me. The pink coat is a bright focal daub in foggy woodland. The hat protects the head. (Hugh wears an ancient silk topper in which he collects mushrooms if there's a lapse in proceedings.) The boots protect the legs from being smashed against a gatepost. The whip is used for opening gates. Even the ceremonial stock has its purpose. "Jumped over a hedge once," Hugh had recounted. "Found Mrs. C. the other side – flat on her back with her leg folded up in a nasty fashion beside her. So I made a splint with her whip, bound up her leg with the stock and she was right as rain."

Recalling all this, my nausea took a swirling turn round my stomach.

171

We left home. We splashed through the ford and plodded up the steep road that climbs the easterly face of Creech Hill, then winds round to Lamyatt and Milton Clevedon where the meet was to be held.

Beyond straggly brown hedges made sluttish with wild clematis, a few Friesian heifers tore at the bleached January pasture. A white-faced Hereford bull with a copper ring through his nose peered down at our slow progress. Bathsheba made a series of disgruntled sounds about the gradient of the hill.

As we drew nearer the meet and passed a few parked horse boxes, I awaited some change in her carriage. When it came, an awakening that travelled right through her, I laughed and ran a hand down her mane. *She* knew what it was all about.

The village is sited two-thirds of the way up a hill that strictly adjoins Creech Hill and is called Lamyatt Beacon – a flat-topped, sheep-shorn promontory where there are signs of modest earthworks. Below, the vale opens up wide and sweeping, dipping to Spargrove at its lowest point and rising to hills that fold away at their highest and furthest in Mendip country.

On that morning at that time, little of it could be seen. The valley was a cold bowl of fog. After the horn had sounded to move off, we climbed into the thinner atmosphere above us, the horses picking their way carefully up the steep, rutted incline. And there we seemed to stand at uncomfortable angles for an age while huntsman and hounds became disembodied noises in the fog below. A cold wind sliced across the top of the hill making Bathsheba restless. I could feel her boiling up a store of energy ready for the signal movement that could start a headlong rush downhill.

"Stay close!" came the cry. But it was hard to keep one's eye on the smears of scarlet as we slithered down into the cloud, across the road, through a farmyard and down again into the muffled valley.

A group of us became separated from those doing the

serious work and I would have dawdled around for ever not knowing what to do next had Bathsheba's ears not been sharply swivelled towards some guiding point of activity well wrapped in fog. She trotted down the road to Lamyatt with no encouragement from me and as the fog melted I could see, above me, in a sudden rush of clear winter sunshine, hounds streaming up to the top of the Beacon followed by most of the field. All but one straggling hound vanished from sight round the far side of the hill and, unable to catch them up for a moment, I stayed down on the road with the foot followers scanning the hill top for movement. The solitary hound picked himself up and loped horizontally westwards across the hill at the very moment a fox emerged running eastwards at an arrow's pace towards him. They collided head on. Both sat down momentarily, shook themselves, then set off in private pursuit towards the dense crest of woodland on top of Creech Hill. "Did you see that! Did you see that, eh!"

Old men who'd watched hounds for fifty years and more turned to one another amazed. They raised their caps to scratch their heads to make sure all was as it should be.

"Never seen anything like it in all my born days!" cried Mr. Carver, seizing the gate to stop himself falling over with laughter. "Just wait till I tell them what they've missed!"

I was told I was lucky to witness such a thing. I didn't realise just how privileged I was until I'd hunted several times without setting eyes on a fox at all. It's rather hard to judge the awkard question as to whether pursuing foxes is something done out of primeval blood lust when you don't actually see one ahead of you. The excitement is real enough as the cry of hounds swells and drives your horse forward under you. But the sharpening of the pulse at that moment has, I think, more to do with the flying pace, the exultant spring of your horse than it has to do with any longing to kill the unseen creature way out in front of the pack. Most foxes in fact escape.

Really to see things, you need to stay with the old men who go on foot. They are the ones who know the land like

173

the inside of their head. They even know individual foxes and where they hole up and which course they are likely to take. It's the old men who know which hilltops offer the best view. What they, what all true huntsmen love to see is not the death of the fox, but the way hounds work, observing the quickness and purpose of a hound on to the scent, noting his deductions as he follows the confused trail of a creature more artful and faster than himself. The old men will tell you admiringly of the strategems a fox can devise. "Saw one run right up over a barn roof once," Mr. Chivers, the Water Board man told me. He and Mr. Crabbe can nearly always be found high on a hill overlooking a drawn covert. Mr. Crabbe went into France with the cavalry in 1916 and now, at seventy-eight, goes out hunting on his motor bike every day he can.

The only kill I was ever to see that winter I saw when I went on foot. A patch of kale was being drawn. Suddenly, ten feet or so away from me, a fox broke out of the dense green leaves. Hounds were on to him immediately and Ken, the huntsman, stood by in an instant with a pistol ready should there be any lingering. There wasn't. The high note of hounds rose and subsided. There was a warm unpleasant smell of meat and I felt sick. But it was swift.

The vale cleared.

Far to the west rose the small blue pyramid of Glastonbury Tor. North of us, forming the immediate rim of the valley, lay the hills of Batcombe and Westcombe, surmounted by a small Iron Age fort.

We clattered down glassy-steep Carrot Hill to the old manor of Spargrove which looks deserted, but isn't. There *are* people there. Occasionally a wooden door scrapes over the flagstones. Sometimes you see a solitary figure in a field. The women don't speak. Their cattle roam loose all the year round, bulls and cows together. The land is poor and the mill wheel is silent. The moat runs deep round the house. The first time I ever rode Bathsheba down Carrot Hill she trembled all over and refused to move beyond a point in the

174

lane. Later someone told me that when their grandfather was a boy, a young lad, a simpleton, had murdered one of his tormentors there.

We jumped nothing that morning. Bathsheba, fightingly eager to go on, wasn't really fit enough and I turned her for home after a couple of hours. Back at Milton Clevedon we paused and stood awhile looking down below us at the remainder of the field. They passed through the valley, small figures trailing after an untidy spread of hounds. Here and there, a deer started up and bounded across the open fields unhindered.

A few weeks later I was to stand there again watching the field I had not left this time but lost, through shameful overconfidence.

The field had become split down in the valley. I found myself in the group furthest away from hounds who were on the far side of the river. Thinking I knew this piece of country well enough and now totally trusting of Bathsheba's ability to jump anything and carry me safely with her, I jumped a hedge while the ladies in the group fiddled over the catch on the gate. Strictly, one is only allowed to jump hedges when hounds are running. Since I couldn't even see them it was a point of etiquette I wasn't competent to judge. Smartly, we cut across country. I was certain we could either ford or jump the river at some point but as I searched frantically for a suitable crossing place, the immaculate ladies I had left behind, their bowlers set at a disdainful angle, caught up, passed behind me and trotted neatly over a wooden bridge some two fields further downstream. Determined not to be left embarrassingly far behind I pushed Bathsheba forward into the narrow stretch of green water dimly conscious that the far bank was some six feet high but just about negotiable. I hadn't allowed for the softness of the river bed. Bathsheba sank into it above the knee, effectively increasing the height of the bank by two feet and giving herself a sticky, difficult base from which to attempt it. She tried and slithered back. Again she made a tremendous effort. With a majestic splash-

175

ing we slid back into the water. *Come on*, I urged (I think not silently). *Come on!*

And she made it. With a supreme effort she clawed her way upward as I slid further and further down her back, blind to a low branch that overhung the bank. Some instinct – to protect my head I imagine – made me throw my arms up, dropping the reins. I found myself clinging to the branch. Bathsheba passed between my legs and cantered on leaving me dangling like a weather-stained effigy in a gallows tree.

It was due punishment for my impertinence for thinking I knew the lie of that particular stretch better than the bowler-hatted ladies who must have floundered through it on small ponies some forty years before. They said nothing. There was no need.

If I were to hunt for the rest of my life it would be impossible for me ever to know each gap, each shallow stretch of water, the one unwired piece of fence in miles of enclosure or the badger track that forms a path beneath the bracken in what seems to be impenetrable copse.

The most passionate enthusiasts will hunt two or three times a week. For most farmers or farming families the winter is their slackest time and once the milking is done, they labour over their horses. But my life has a different pattern and I didn't have time even for one day a week that particular January when labour outweighed leisure by quite serious proportions. I seemed to be endlessly rising at six, milking, mucking out, catching the seven-thirty train to London with my face unwashed and my hair screwed up under a head-scarf trying to remove the grime from my hands with British Rail soap and a scrubbing brush in order to do some programme or other; arranging for someone else to collect the children from school, arranging for the children to feed the animals, arranging for John to squeak home and feed the children. The house, scoured for Christmas, relapsed into its customary squalor, letters pended, green crumbs accumulated in the bread bin and I became more and more anxious

176

about the likelihood of ever bringing Athene into fruitful conjunction with the billy.

Quite deliberately I'd delayed Athene's visit to the billy. Imagining I was more organised now, I'd thought to stagger my kiddings so as to have milk all the year round without a break rather than have all the goats dried off at the same time. So, like women awaiting their turn for the palmist's tent, they'd gone one behind the other after an excited interval. With Athene, however, I never seemed to get the timing quite right. She ate bracken again and came so near to death she was too weak to visit the billy. By the time she was stronger it was halfway through January when the goat's period of season wanes. If I missed this time, I'd very likely have her dry and unproductive for a full year. The consequence of it all was that I spent an undue amount of time peering over my silent typewriter through the window into the paddock below for a promising sign of her readiness.

There was a mild wagging of the tail one darkening, snowy afternoon.

"Well," said the Yarlington billy owner over the phone (he sounded dubious), "he hasn't been too well. Never mind," he added on reflection, "perhaps this'll put him on his feet again. You'd better come right over."

I stuck Athene in the back of my old Morris where she settled in pleasant anticipation of a drive and we rattled over to Yarlington. Skidding over the snowy yard I halted and we staggered out in search of the billy.

A pitiable sight awaited us. This wasn't the snarling, trumpeting creature I knew at all. He lay in a nest of straw and tried to rise as we approached.

"Do you think he *can*?" I wondered.

"He'll have a go," said the Yarlington billy owner sadly, "if he's able." And tenderly he encouraged the shaggy animal.

It was a valiant performance. The billy stumbled to his feet, uttered faint appreciative noises, tried to mount Athene and fell flat on his face.

"Oh dear," murmured his owner, rubbing the sinking

177

animal's neck. "I tell you what, we'll try his son. He's only a youngster but I think he's ready."

We fought our way through the dark with a torch to another shed and tried the billy's son. Athene attempted to flatten him against the wooden wall.

"I don't think this is going to work," I said.

The Yarlington billy owner gave me the name of somebody at Marple with a young billy goat and I rang their number that night to make an appointment for the following morning.

My Morris drew up in front of a stately home. Athene and I approached the handsome portico and rang a huge brass bell. As we waited for somebody to come to the door, Athene peed all over the grand semi-circular step.

"Awfully sorry," I apologised cravenly to the figure in the doorway. It was Georgie Fame clearly not wanting to be recognised. I'd always had rather a soft spot for Georgie Fame.

We let our two goats sniff one another. Athene lunged and the billy, retreating behind his owner's legs, refused to emerge again. I said I thought Athene was just being provocative. "It's a bit desperate," I added, entreatingly. "It may be her last season."

So we stood there aimlessly in the cold and the wind for a bit longer, but it was useless. The billy quavered against his owner's legs and avoided Athene's yellow eye. Georgie Fame looked faintly ashamed of his billy.

I tore back home and, spying Henry at the garage as I passed, called out, "Know of any billies nearby, Henry? Time's running out!"

"Have you tried the Batcombe billy?"

"Batcombe billy? No. Where is he?"

"Behind the pub," called Henry as I ground into second gear and lurched off.

Driving into the pub yard I *thought* I saw a buffalo hanging over the top of a lower stable door. Getting out of the car and looking more closely I saw it was a billy, a quite

178

exceptionally large brown billy, whose feet hung over the door like two large Alpine cow bells.

"Crumbs," I breathed in awe and pulling Athene out of the back of the car, I let her take in the prospect for herself. Her ears pivoted forward like alarmed radar needles.

I knocked on the back door of the pub and a harassed-looking man clutching four hot water bottles opened it. I pointed at my goat and explained the exigencies of the situation. He looked distraught. "Can you manage yourself?" he pleaded, "I have the whole family in bed with 'flu and I can't . . ."

"Oh, *please* . . . I'm sorry. Not to worry. No, truly . . ." I stepped back with a self-confident salute, my stomach leaking to my feet and advanced across the yard to the stable.

Keeping Athene carefully between myself and the billy, I edged into the stable and made a number of soothing noises. The billy leapt. Athene and I sank to the ground under the weight of him and wriggled away. He wasn't, I realised, being unpleasant. Just friendly and keen. But Athene raced round and round the confined space dragging me after her with the billy in parallel pursuit. She wasn't having any. After ten minutes of heated activity, I gave up and squeezed out of the stable again.

"All right?" called the publican.

"Er, thank you so much," I said. "She seems not to be in season any longer. I'm sorry to have taken up your time."

He raised a hot water bottle in farewell. "*Any* time!" he responded.

We smelt appalling.

No sooner had I washed and returned to the typewriter than I heard the lascivious blare of a goat in season. Not Athene. Nefertiti this time.

"Too bad!" I yelled from the window. "Wait your turn!" And I pounded away at a commissioned piece on The Greatest Influence Of My Life.

Even without frost the countryside looked frozen into stillness. The trees were stiff and rusty, the elms in particular with

their shaving-brush tops seemed imprisoned in sleep. And
then a weak spread of February sunshine would suddenly
turn the pale and weary colours of winter into something
gentler, a fragility that suggested all would be unlocked in
a matter of weeks.

Muck-spreading started and a pungent smell was loosed
everywhere. Then ploughing and the gulls came inland to
see what pickings there were.

For the moment, though, until March, the catkins hung
in the hedge a dry, dull ochre colour. Not the colour of new
life at all.

I saw a big dog fox at Hook Valley. Big and gold. We
jumped endlessly that day. Bathsheba never stopped – indeed, was so acutely anxious to be first over everything I was
frowned upon once by the Field Master whose privilege it is
to risk his neck first over a fence. She kept going, putting her
head down and making for gaps where she thought she could
overtake other more sedate animals. Even when she was utterly exhausted after a long run and her flanks pumped up and
down, she somehow found her second wind and when I turned
her for home, she curved her body pleadingly towards the
departing field somewhere discovering the energy to go even
better than before. Her zest was enormous. She was as happy
as a creature can be. On ordinary days when we set out for
a ride, she began hopefully enough but soon let me know
by the feel of her back and slump of her head that she considered herself cheated. But the night before a hunting day
when I washed and bandaged her tail and pulled her mane
to a tidy length, she trembled all over with intense anticipation. Only for hunting was she willingly prepared to leave
Narcissus and, although they exchanged delighted whinnying
screams whenever she returned home muddy and wet from
a day out, she would have stayed with hounds until nightfall
had I let her. In fact, just once, on a day when she lost two
shoes and I had to take her home before she felt she'd had
anything remotely like her fair share of pleasure, she led
quietly into the trailer, then tried her old trick of running

back when she was tied. Three times she did it while the re-knotted rope grew shorter and shorter. Eventually I had to go into the saloon bar of the pub where I'd parked and ask if a man would mind standing behind me (a request which brought forth coarse laughter and at least five men) before she was prepared to be loaded for home. I couldn't be angry with her however much a fool I felt. Nothing but a reluctance to leave hounds had made her misbehave. She had broken backwards but then had stood patiently waiting in the pub car park to be caught and re-mounted, that was all. There was no vice in her.

The last fragments of hostility and suspicion, that once underlay her fundamental sweetness of nature, evaporated with hunting. She was full of gaiety, full of trust. Her wisdom and courage out hunting was so great that she taught me to be brave. Under her supervision I dared things I would never have countenanced in cold blood. She educated me. Even my riding improved. There is a saying about jumping in the horse world – it is this: "Throw your heart over first and your horse will follow."

It was the other way round in our partnership. I flung myself in the wake of her bold and generous heart and she never failed me. Once, as we flew over a wide thorn hedge, I saw that the girl who had taken off ahead of us had jumped short and slithered into the ditch on the far side. As we jumped she and her horse were scrambling out of the ditch directly in our path. Bathsheba slewed in mid-air, avoided them, landed perfectly and galloped on without hesitation. She was, for all her size, as nimble as a cat.

As spring advances and the valleys are sown, hunting slows down. It stays up in the hill country and then, in March, restricts itself to slower, beautiful days in the woodland.

Because of a minor accident only one day's hunting was left to us in March before the season ended entirely. Out exercising, I'd cantered over a dip in a field which turned out to be an overgrown slurry pond. Bathsheba had gone straight down into thick black water which closed over my thighs.

181

As she'd struggled in the sinking mud I'd thrown myself off her back to free her of my weight just at the moment she'd wrenched herself round. Our joint movement had knocked me under the water and under her. Twice I sank down spitting mud. The second time she had trodden on my hands pinning me down. Fortunately the mud was so deep and squelchy my fingers weren't broken. In fact there was no feeling in them at all and having caught her and examined her carefully to make sure she was unhurt, I had been able to ride her home. Once I'd washed her down, rubbed her dry, rugged and fed her, fetched the children, made tea, and sat through a committee meeting being held in our house, I passed out. For the next few days my fingers were too painful to hold the reins and I forfeited two possible outings in the woods. It made the last day's hunting all the more to be savoured. After this, Bathsheba, whose new coat was already growing through, was to be turned away to rest and summer out with her growing colt.

It dawned perfectly, a cool, bright day. Daffodils sang out from the gardens we passed as we trotted towards the meet in Brewham Forest. The primroses which had flowered since January still shone in the banks.

Only a handful of people bother to go on woodland days. The small company and the slower pace are pleasant because they afford a better opportunity of watching hounds work. And I love the forest. Seen from a distance, from Charley Hill, it's a thick, black coniferous pelt broken only by the sentinel pink of Alfred's Tower but within, it's delicious. Light shafts through the bare larches and warms fragrance out of the fallen needles. The darkness of some parts of the forest, the way its paths circle up and down, round and round, make you lose all sense of direction and then it can be an eerie place, curiously birdless and silent (except for the occasional pigeon that flaps out of the trees). Hoofbeats are muffled in the soft, brown mould. Even the leaping deer pass soundlessly between the tall trees. Then, quite suddenly,

you can break out of the darkness and emerge on a steep sun-
lit bank, its descent thick with bracken and tiny young
conifers and the light comes as a relief, a great pale blaze
that spreads over the trees as they slide away beneath you
exposing the little fields and farms beyond and – furthest
away of all – the sleeping form of Creech Hill.

We stood on such a slope, the huntsmen moving beneath us,
scarlet coats bobbing above the sandy bracken, hounds almost entirely obscured by it. Their cries – the preliminary
whining babble of hounds, the yelping commands of the
Whip – echoed through the forest.

"Hee-uw! Hee-uw! Hee-oy! Hee-oy!"

It is rare to find a fox in the forest. While hounds searched,
the hunt terrier took himself off in personal pursuit of a rabbit.

Bathsheba fretted quietly. All waiting made her impatient.
Apart from the suppressed clinking of metal bits we fell
silent, senses stretched for the altered note of a hound giving
tongue.

A few yards away from me, in deeper bracken, Henry
Barker sat on his great broad mare, Bonny. He pressed his
fingers to his lips and beckoned me to come and look. A
roebuck nestled in the tawny undergrowth only feet away,
motionless and calm as he gazed back.

(It was Henry who had insisted I have one of his Indian
gamecocks when he heard the fox had taken our cockerel.
He took us into a whitewashed stable where twelve vivid
birds had flown about from perch to perch and I'd been allowed to choose one with a golden ruff and lustred plumage.
Most of the people I met out hunting were as good-hearted
as Henry and Hugh. Many had a mad kind of courage I
found very endearing. Elderly people in surgical collars or
slings who were prepared to have a go at any obstacle.)

The huntsman, below, blew his horn and led us away from
this draw, deeper into the woods. Gradually our pace increased and Bathsheba tried to resist my restraining hand.
You have to be careful in the woods, ducking branches or
the brambles that tear at your hair and face. As we climbed

183

along narrowing paths the going became more difficult. In the thick tangle of undergrowth it wasn't easy to see where the path lay. Several times I had to rely on Bathsheba quickly to negotiate a concealed culvert or unexpectedly boggy dip. Twice, as we twisted through the bushes and bracken, she stumbled. Although she strove valiantly to keep up and tried to ignore my efforts to steady her, I could sense a perceptible difference in her. Her spirit strained after the others as she struggled uphill and then, uncertainly down, her eagerness making her clumsy as she tried to do more than her legs would perform. I reined her in after a good level run when I could tell that it wasn't the going but something else that was troubling her. Her head, against her own best will, drooped briefly.

Reluctantly, she let me turn her homewards raising her head to whinny after the others whose rustling movements she yearningly heard. A distant horn made her dance.

I took her off the Phenylbutazone straight away. Within twenty-four hours she was fearfully lame. She was turned out for three weeks complete rest, grazing alongside Cissy. Their fine summer coats began to grow. Cissy fattened quickly, the lanky, baby lines taking on a more powerful and mature form. As they worked their way across the tender new grass, Bathsheba remained as lame as ever. The way she rested her forelegs made me anxious.

There was good news, too. John had started work at his new job in Bristol. With him living at home full time there was more talk, even more to do, more digging, cooking, washing – less time to spend just hanging over the gate watching the animals in general. It was Bathsheba I watched for signs of improvement as she slowly cropped her way over the grass. As she moved away from me, shoulder to shoulder with her greedy son, flicking her tail gently to suggest a proper distance between them, I had a strong and curious sense that something had been fulfilled. As though with John home, she was retiring from the bond we'd shared. Wise old thing, she knew from the change in routine the season had ended. The dream was done.

Twitch kidded. Under a leafless gooseberry bush she gave birth to triplets, two billies and a nanny. Forsythia blazed a brave yellow in the cottage gardens and over their walls, the rock plants turned a springy green.

The vet came to de-horn the kids and put down one billy. The other was being kept as a possible replacement for the Yarlington billy who had finally died. While these various annual tasks were being done, I asked the vet if he would look at Bathsheba whose lameness was no better. Carefully he felt around the joints of her front feet, lifting them, bending them. At length he stood up.

"I think it's ringbone," he said.

My very worst fears confirmed, I felt my heart sink.

I *had* wondered. Heavily, I thought back over her history, the showjumping she was said to have sickened of, the doubtful dealer, the vet whose certificate had never arrived, the recurrent lameness, the 'shoulder' trouble. I thought of the many, many times, I'd bothered anyone I knew who had a practised eye with my doubtful questions. Is she all right, do you think, I'd pressed, and they'd looked and judged and decided that she was fine or a bit unfit or a bit lazy or having me on. And all the time I'd wondered. But then, when I'd finally succumbed and taken her hunting, her intense and buoyant happiness had swept all the doubts away. They'd been over-anxious imaginings, I'd thought. Ridiculous motherly fussing.

I looked at her as she stood patiently beside us and grieved.

"You can't do anything for it, can you?" I asked rhetorically, knowing the answer perfectly well. Ringbone is a build up of arthritic deposits on the pastern joint. It is hopeless.

"I want to be sure," I said fiercely. "I want her X-rayed." And I'm afraid I wept in front of him.

A terrible fortnight elapsed before I could take her to be X-rayed and during that time Wideawake, the winner of the

Badminton Horse Trials, dropped dead in the ring after his triumphant circuit. It was disclosed that he had been given Phenylbutazone the night before the cross-country phase and immediately a bitter debate was waged about the drug and its uses. Much of what was said was spiteful and ignorant. Those who think the sport is cruel seized the opportunity to attack the practice of 'doping', as it was described. I don't for one moment imagine that Wideawake died as a result of having the drug, but out of the raging correspondence in the press one or two salient facts emerged. One, that the drug contains cortisone which can, over a period of prolonged usage, make the bones brittle. Secondly, that it can, beyond any question, by masking the pain of a complaint when a horse is being worked, aggravate the condition seriously. Reading all this as the days passed, my sorrow was deepened by guilt.

Bathsheba and Narcissus were put out in Jack Hopkins' field where the grass was more plentiful, and day after day I sat on Charley Hill opposite, watching her. She rested first one foot, then the other. When Cissy cannoned into her after one of his exuberant circles, she flinched visibly. She looked old. It was very hard to bear.

The X-rays were carried out and confirmed the vet's original findings. I wept again.

"You could breed from her," he suggested gently. "Or just leave her to see her days out in the field."

So I put her back in the field and again I sat and watched her shift her weight from foot to foot. Sometimes she huddled herself into an uncomfortable-looking position to ease the pain. I didn't know what to do.

One evening I went with a pocketful of oats and stood on the slope above them calling them both. With a squeal of delight, Cissy galloped to me and burrowed his muzzle in the palm of my hand but his mother simply stood and looked at me, unwilling to move.

She ate gladly enough when I went to her. I stroked her and pulled her ears and knew that the greatest cruelty of all

186

would be for me to keep her to save myself the pain of being without her.

I called round at the surgery and asked the vet to come and put her down at the end of the week.

I find it hard to describe the agony of those days. I hope to God I never feel as treacherous towards a human being as I felt towards that grey mare whose dear, funny shape and bruised personality had become a deep and reflected part of me. I was about to break the trust she had, at last, so unreservedly come to place in me.

On the appointed Friday I brought her into the stable and talked to her as calmly as I was able. She rubbed her forehead against my shoulder and picked a few oats from my hand. At noon, the slaughterer's van arrived and parked in the yard.

"You'd have got a decent price for her if you'd brought the mare straight to us," the driver advised me, not unkindly.

"I know," I said.

The vet came and I led her out on to the lawn. In the field, out of sight, Cissy whinnied.

I rubbed her neck as she backed away, her fear of men rising instinctively to the surface. "It's all right, my love, steady now . . ." I murmured and scratched her withers as comfortably as I could.

There was a loud bang and a smell of burning. She dropped to her knees her large eye dark with shock.

"You go now." The vet took the rope from my hand.

I went indoors and let my heart break.

I cried until I was dried up with sadness.

Epilogue

SOMETIMES, THE COUNTRYSIDE CAN SEEM QUITE CRUEL IN its lack of ceremonial pause.

Twenty-four hours had not elapsed before Narcissus – removed to a neighbour's field – was pursued by a jealous pony into a hut and through a glass window, splitting his head open. The vet returned and delicately stitched him above the eye.

The day was warm. Fine enough to put the two scrawny kids Hollyhock had lately delivered with bawling hardship outside in the field. They started making serious demands on their mother's small udder while she tore raptly at the grass. The Scraggies, our once debilitated battery hens, earned a reprieve by laying their first egg. Their plumage shone. They had become healthy, contented, fearless and unusually affectionate hens who ran and hopped up and down on your foot clamouring for grain.

That day – the last in April – the cuckoo arrived.

Calling the dog to heel I make my evening tour. We pass leafless plum trees now fixed with small, sparse, festive stars. In the back lane up to Charley Hill, the satiny tongues of wild garlic are early lapping the bank this year. The last of the sunlight unrolling itself at a low angle down the hill makes the grass appear quite drunkenly green, so sharp a colour that it hurts the eyes.

I can't ever recall a more beautiful spring. The leaves that have appeared at last on the elder and hawthorn are edibly green and there are tight pink buds amid the apple leaves. But the first to flower has been the blackthorn that lies in the old laid hedges. Here, from the top of Charley, I can see its sprays curving sideways like flying spume on the crests of the hills.

Carefully, I mark my stations. First the slumbering dome of Creech Hill. Then the long incline down to Coombe Farm, which stands in a cleavage of the hills, a doll's house made of stone the colour of fleece. The eye rises a little, then passes down the reclining line of trees that leads to the row of pale yellow houses, each set at a different angle, each proprietor of a different view. They stand above the tumble of houses in the town, above the church tower and its chiming clock.

The warmest pool of remaining light lies on the mound belonging to the dovecote. By some kind accident of geography this small hill has in its gift both the first and the last light of day.

My shadow reaches thirty feet downhill, an inaccurately narrow blue pointer directed back towards the house. One corner of the roof is visible beside the massive copper beech tree which, always late into leaf, is showing its first rusty flush.

Follow the line further, away to the east, beyond the green triangle of Cogley Woods to Brewham. On this particular evening the forest is like a blue cloak draped over the hill.

189

It's odd, but no matter how often the colour of the massed foliage changes, the rosy brick of Alfred's Tower, which breaks above it, is always exact. Distance doesn't alter it at all.

The dog sits beside me, head alert as I follow the line on round and silently make the lovely enumeration of place names . . . Redlynch, Godminster, Shepton Montague, Bratton Seymour . . . between here and Bratton are a thousand small fields studded with black and white cows. One of those fields belongs to the Holgates, the only part of their farm visible this side of the high ridge.

On then, down the long spine of Trendle Lane, on to Wyke Champflower, and the coppery sky that lingers above Glastonbury. The journey is complete. I am back where I began with the eternally sleeping beast of Creech.

Somewhere a woodpecker taps at a trunk. Milking must be over and Eddie's cattle returned to their fields along Lady-well, for I can hear the boys on their motorbikes down the lane, the note of their engines changing as they jolt over the dried and rutted mud.

A cow, whose calf has been lately taken from her, moans persistently. Like her, I mourn a lost creature – and something less definable as well. I mourn a residual fragment of childhood that has ended with her death.

April, 'the cruellest month', is ended. May, begun.